Modernit,

To Asteris Stefan

Modernity
Understanding the Present

Peter Wagner

Polity

First published in 2012 by Polity Press

Polity Press
65 Bridge Street
Cambridge CB2 1UR, UK

Polity Press
350 Main Street
Malden, MA 02148, USA

ISBN-13: 978-0-7456-5290-0
ISBN-13: 978-0-7456-5291-7(pb)

A catalogue record for this book is available from the British Library.

Typeset in 11 on 13 pt Sabon
by Toppan Best-set Premedia Limited
Printed and bound in Great Britain by the MPG Books Group

The publisher has used its best endeavours to ensure that the URLs for external websites referred to in this book are correct and active at the time of going to press. However, the publisher has no responsibility for the websites and can make no guarantee that a site will remain live or that the content is or will remain appropriate.

Every effort has been made to trace all copyright holders, but if any have been inadvertently overlooked the publisher will be pleased to include any necessary credits in any subsequent reprint or edition.

For further information on Polity, visit our website: www.politybooks.com

Contents

Preface   vii

Part I   Re-theorizing Modernity   1

1 Retrieving Modernity's Past, Understanding
   Modernity's Present   3

2 Changing Views of Modernity: From
   Convergence and Stability to Plurality
   and Transformations   11

3 Successive Modernities: Crisis, Criticism and
   the Idea of Progress   28

4 Disentangling the Concept of Modernity: Time,
   Action and Problems to Be Solved   64

Part II   Analysing Contemporary Modernity   79

5 The Link between Capitalism and Democracy
   Reconsidered   81

6 European and Non-European Trajectories of
   Modernity Compared   107

7 Violence and Justice in Global Modernity:
Reflections on South Africa with
World-Sociological Intent   119

8 Towards a World Sociology of Modernity   150

References   171
Index   183

Preface

Fifty years ago, the globe was neatly divided into three areas: the First World of liberal–democratic industrial capitalism, the Second World of Soviet-style socialism, and the Third World of so-called developing countries. Within the First World, there was a clear view about how to understand the present of the time. The First World only was composed of 'modern societies', which were superior to all others because they had institutionalized freedom and had developed an institutional differentiation according to functional needs. In this view, the Second World societies had embarked on an erroneous path which they could only maintain at the risk of perishing in the system competition with the First World; and the societies of the Third World were in the process of following the First one in processes of 'modernization and development'. Only First World societies, thus, were modern in the sense of being in their own time. The Second World had aimed to create its own, specific future but necessarily failed; and the Third World needed to catch up to reach the present. This was the time when our sociological thinking about 'modern society' and 'modernization' emerged as an extremely coherent attempt at understanding the present of that time.

But it is no longer our time – and arguably no longer our modernity. The world has changed considerably and much beyond the sociological imagination of anyone writing in the 1960s.

The western societies of the 1960s were 'industrial societies', built on the innovations of the so-called Second Industrial Revolution, with electrical engineering, chemical engineering and the combustion engine, and the possibility of a 'post-industrial society' just beginning to be considered. Now, we speak of knowledge societies in the wake of a Third Industrial Revolution based on electronic engineering and producing the new information and communication technologies that enhance global interconnectedness.

During the 1960s, governments believed in crisis-free national economies that were steered by Keynesian demand management techniques. Now, most of the economic policy institutions of that time have been dismantled in the wake of a new belief in market self-regulation, and the global capitalism that resulted from this change has already entered into a deep crisis, comparable only to the Great Depression of 1929, which many economists thought was the last one ever. And, across the last half-century, we have also witnessed the rise of regional economies to world competitiveness – first Japan, then Taiwan and South Korea, now China, to mention only a few – that are not based in the cultural context of Protestantism and its social ethic which many sociologists had considered a requirement.

The 1960s were the peak of the era of decolonization, witnessing the rapid dismantling of European empires, but it was expected that the new states and societies would emulate the western model and, given that they were 'late', would keep lagging somewhat behind. Now, we know that liberation from western dominance can also mean a fundamental challenge to the model of modernization, as in the case of the Iranian Revolution of 1979 and the rise of Islamism, or at least the emergence of distinct varieties of modernity, for the creation of which local problem-solving is more important than the look to the West. The new powers in the world – such as China, India, Brazil and South Africa – emerge from different historical trajectories, such as experiences of a regional version of communism, colonial domination, extreme inequality in an entrenched oligarchic setting or apartheid, and their 'modernities' are bound to be shaped by those experiences, and sometimes now their choices are seen as models to be emulated elsewhere.

Of the changes over the last fifty years, democratization is the one that was most predicted – modern societies were supposed to be democratic polities – but both the speed of change after a long period of persistent authoritarianism in the world (benevolently viewed by western powers, we should add) and its consequences were highly unexpected. Political scientists now speak of 'waves of democratization' as something self-evident, and they refer to the end of military dictatorships in Southern Europe in the 1970s, followed by South Korea and Latin America, and then the demise of Soviet-style socialism in Eastern Europe from 1989, the end of apartheid in South Africa during the same years, and now the democratic movements in Northern Africa and the Middle East, which still have to bring democratic regimes about. Two aspects tend to be forgotten when seeing something like a natural process at work in democratization. First, the world of the 1960s appeared neat and stable largely because it was undemocratic. The United States of America feared democracy in Latin America; Europe feared democracy in the Muslim Maghreb; the 'modern' Kemalist government in Turkey feared Islamic and Kurdish expression in its own society; Israel feared democracy in Palestine; and these fears are far from over. When global modernity becomes truly based on collective self-determination, the world will have changed. Second, democracy in the 1960s meant collective self-determination within the well-defined boundaries of nation-states, and the assumption was that such societies could indeed determine their own destiny because they were separate and distinguishable from other societies in the world. Now we may have more democratically constituted societies, but global interdependence may mean that those collectivities have very little to indeed decide and determine.

In sum, technology, economy and politics have changed beyond recognition in the world over the past half-century. If a part of the world was seen as a 'modern society' then, its modernity was radically different from the modernity of our present. If other parts of the world then were seen as having to face 'modernization', they have interpreted this challenge often in very different ways from those expected. For these reasons, an attempt at understanding our present time cannot rely on the tools and concepts of even such a seemingly recent past as that of the 1960s. This book thus aims to provide a renewed reflection about modernity with a view to better understanding our present time.

For a long time, it was common to think that modernity originated in the West and that it opened up a new and better era in the history of humanity. This book returns to these claims but discusses them in the light of the current global nature of modernity. Modernity's claims and expectations have become inescapable in evermore walks of life and for many more people than before. In the course of their realization and diffusion, however, these claims and expectations have also been radically transformed. Newly arising issues will need to be discussed by posing the following questions:

- Sociologists and philosophers have long maintained that there is – indeed, that there can be – only a single model of modernity. However, modern institutions and practices have been transformed over time, and furthermore there is now a plurality of forms of modern socio-political organization. What does this entail for our idea of progress, or, in other words, for our hope that the future world can be better than the present one?
- Modernity was based on the hope of freedom and reason, but it created the institutions of contemporary capitalism and democracy. How does the freedom of the citizen relate to the freedom of the buyer and seller

today? And what does disaffection with capitalism and
democracy entail for the sustainability of modernity?
• All nuance and broadening notwithstanding, our
concept of modernity is in some way inextricably tied
to the history of Europe and the West. How can we
compare different forms of modernity in a 'symmetric',
non-biased or non-Eurocentric way? How can we
develop a world sociology of modernity?

The reflections in this book are based on an approach to
'modernity as experience and interpretation' which I had
tried to elaborate as a rather novel way of linking comparative–historical sociology to social and political philosophy.
The questions above were in the background of my earlier
writing (Wagner 2008), but they had not yet been explicitly
addressed. The answers I now hope to give to them can be
found in this book. The current constellation of modernity
forces us to reconsider our ways of theorizing it. This will
be done in the first part of the book. The second part will
embark on analyses of key aspects of our present time with
the help of a revised understanding of modernity, as elaborated on in the first part.

Chapter 1 discusses the global nature of modernity by
way of a brief review of key ideas of modernity from
the point of view of the present. The thinking about modernity has always aimed at the global and the universal.
Modernity was seen as normatively and functionally superior to other forms of socio-political organization. Universal
claims were made in its name, and its worldwide diffusion
was expected. It is now, however, in our era of so-called
globalization, of radical time–space compression, that these
claims and expectations become truly inescapable. But they
have to be read differently after centuries of experience of
translating them into socio-political practices. Subsequently,
chapter 2 elaborates systematically on the recent change
in perceptions of modernity. It focuses on two key issues:
rather than seeing 'modern societies' converge to a single
institutional expression, many observers now identify a

persistent plurality of modern forms of socio-political organization. Secondly, rather than seeing 'modern societies' as basically stable once their full institutional expression has been reached, most observers now agree that modernity has been undergoing quite radical change from at least the 1970s onwards.

The new concerns with persistent plurality and possibly profound transformations of modernity open up further questions. Chapter 3 investigates if and how we can sustain the idea of progress that has long informed the debate about modernity if modernity has more than one shape and goes on changing. Finally, chapter 4 suggests that a new understanding of modernity needs to build on the insight in the contingency of historical developments. The history of modernity is not a smooth unfolding of basic ideas and principles as they move towards concretization in historical reality. Rather, it is a struggle over the interpretation of such ideas and principles, a struggle in the course of which central problems of human social life need to be addressed and in which any solution to these problems may engender new problems to be addressed in the future.

The reasoning in the first part of this book uses historical and contemporary examples wherever possible, but it does so with a view to elaborating a novel understanding of modernity. The approach changes in the second part. From chapter 5 onwards, the focus will be on the trajectories of modernity in different parts of the world, with a view to seeing clearly how modern world-views have changed societies and how we have arrived at the current constellation of modernity. Conceptual reasoning will now be in the service of understanding historical change.

Chapter 5 explores the relationship between what arguably have been the core institutions of modernity – or imaginaries of modern institutions – over the past two centuries, namely, capitalism and democracy. It will demonstrate that, whatever 'logic' of capitalism and of democracy there may be, the political and economic history of those two centuries is better grasped by focusing on the articulation between the two phenomena, on the challenges that capitalism posed for democracy and those that democracy posed for capitalism. The aim of this exercise is to provide an understanding of the peculiar situation of the present in which a globally diffused capitalism seems to be aligned with unstoppable processes of 'democratization', but in which both political and economic institutions are highly crisis-ridden.

From the analysis of core institutions of modernity in chapter 5, our reasoning moves on to systematically explore in chapter 6 the varieties of modern self-understandings that have emerged globally. This chapter begins with the insight into the persistent plurality of modern forms, as discussed in chapter 2, and offers an approach for analysing this plurality comparatively, based on the conceptual reflections in chapter 4. While being global in outlook, the focus of this chapter will be on two 'post-colonial' societies, Brazil and South Africa, that have rarely been studied in terms of modernity and will provide the tools for comparing their 'modernities' with the European one that has traditionally been at the centre of the analysis of modernity. Chapter 7 will deepen the analysis of South Africa. The task of this case study is to show how to address a key question that emerges when we conceive of modernity in plural terms: what are the aspects that all modernities have in common and what marks the singularity of any particular modernity? With these reflections, all the tools are in hand to conclude the book by outlining the contours of a world sociology of modernity that is capable of helping us to understand our present time. This will be done in chapter 8.

This book would not have existed without the occasion that first solicited it, the Nordic Summer University in Tyrifjord, Norway, in July 2009. Therefore, I would like to express my thanks to the organizers, and in particular to Ingerid Straume, for providing the occasion on which to reflect anew about the ways in which social and political thought and research can help understanding of our present condition (an earlier and shorter version of my lectures appeared as the 'summer talks' of NSU). Thanks are also due to Mikael Carleheden for asking for a contribution to an issue of *Distinktion: Scandinavian Journal for Social Theory* on 'successive modernities', which has been the starting point for the reflections in chapter 3. A first version of chapter 2 was written while lecturing at the Université catholique de Louvain-la-Neuve in March 2010, and I would like to thank Jean de Munck for having created this occasion. The thoughts about novel ways of comparing modernities, contained in chapters 4 and 6, have appeared in an early form in an issue of the *European Journal of Social Theory* which was devoted to the work of Johann Arnason who has been a discussant for matters of modernity for more than ten years now. Chapter 8 originated as a contribution to a volume honouring the work of Björn Wittrock to whom the same applies for more than a quarter-century. Chapter 5 goes back to a keynote lecture given at the conference of the International Social Theory Consortium, organized at the University of Sussex in June 2010 by Gerard Delanty and Stephen Turner. Chapter 7 draws on my contribution to the fiftieth anniversary issue of *Social Science Information/ Information sur les sciences sociales*. Parts of chapter 1 also appear in the *Encyclopedia of Globalization*, edited by George Ritzer (2012) and parts of chapter 2 have appeared in the *Handbook of Contemporary Social and Political Theory*, edited by Gerard Delanty and Stephen Turner (2011).

More thanks: work on this book, in particular on the second part, has greatly benefited from funding by the European Research Council for the project 'Trajectories of Modernity' (TRAMOD) under the European Union's Seventh Framework Programme as Advanced Grant no. 249438. The members of the research project contributed to the book through intense discussions of some of the following chapters. At Polity Press, John Thompson and Sarah Lambert received the proposal and accompanied the work on the manuscript with enthusiasm and trust. Two anonymous reviewers for Polity offered observations on imbalances and lacunae that made me revise and, I hope, improve the structure of the book.

If this book differs from my preceding one by having a wider horizon, in both the geographical and the figurative sense, this is to an inestimable extent due to Nathalie Karagiannis.

Bellaterra, 27 June 2011

Part I

Re-theorizing Modernity

1

Retrieving Modernity's Past, Understanding Modernity's Present

The most common – even though far from unproblematic – view about modernity holds that this term refers to a novel kind of society that emerged from a sequence of major transformations in Europe and North America, culminating in the industrial and democratic revolutions of the late eighteenth and early nineteenth centuries. Significantly, this view often entails both that these transformations catapulted Europe (or the West) to the front position in the course of world history and that the thus established western model would diffuse worldwide because of its inherent superiority. Thinking about modernity thus meant thinking about globalization, even though these terms have come into frequent use only since the 1980s and 1990s respectively.

Global – or universal – significance was claimed for European modernity from the very beginning. A key event in the formation of what we consider to be modern Europe was the so-called discovery of the Americas with their hitherto unknown populations, and this event triggered European reflections about the nature of humankind and provided a background to philosophical speculations about the 'state of nature', as in John Locke's *Second Treatise on Government* (1690). From René Descartes's *Discourse on Method* (1637) onwards, Enlightenment thought claimed to have established the very few, but absolutely firm, foundations on which universal knowledge could be erected, most basically freedom and reason. The American and French Revolutions were seen as having inescapably introduced humanity to liberal democracy, based on individual rights and popular sovereignty. Already in his *Democracy in America* of the 1830s, Alexis de Tocqueville considered equal universal suffrage the *telos* of political history. And from Adam Smith's *Wealth of Nations* (1776) to the mid-nineteenth century, political economists claimed to have discovered in market self-regulation an absolutely superior form of economic organization. In the *Communist Manifesto* (1848), Karl Marx and Friedrich Engels provided an image of economic globalization whose evocative power has not been surpassed.

A common basic understanding of modernity underlies this debate, which stretches over more than two centuries and addresses very different aspects of human social life. Modernity is the belief in the freedom of the human being – natural and inalienable, as many philosophers presumed – and in the human capacity to reason, combined with the intelligibility of the world, that is, its amenability to human reason. In a first step towards concreteness, this basic commitment translates into the principles of individual and collective self-determination and in the expectation of ever-increasing mastery of nature and ever more reasonable interaction between human beings. The Declaration of the Rights of Man and of the Citizen (1793), as well as the granting of commercial freedom, can be understood as an application of these underlying principles of modernity, as can the technical transformations captured by the term 'industrial revolution'.

These principles were seen as *universal*, on the one hand, because they contained normative claims to which, one presumed, every human being would subscribe and, on the other, because they were deemed to permit the creation of functionally superior arrangements for major aspects of human social life, most importantly maybe the satisfaction of human needs in market-driven, industrial production and the rational government of collective matters through law-based and hierarchically organized administration. Furthermore, they were seen as *globalizing* in their application because of the interpretative and practical power of normativity and functionality.

None of these claims, however, was straightforwardly accepted. Even though the intellectual commitment to these principles was possibly widespread, considerable doubts existed about the possibility or probability of translating these principles into institutional arrangements without considerable modifications and losses. Among the early critical reflections, only two shall be mentioned. Immanuel Kant was committed to the idea of enlightened and accountable government and expected the republican principle (though not the democratic one) to flourish worldwide. However, he did not believe in what might have been considered the crowning of this process, the creation of a world republic, but argued for the normative superiority of a global federation of republics instead (*On Perpetual Peace*, 1795). Karl Marx's 'critique of political economy' (thus the subtitle of *Capital*, 1867), in turn, undermined the belief that the transformation of the human being into a market agent was based on the principles of liberty and equality, as political economy had suggested. Rather, this novel social formation, which he referred to as bourgeois society, divided humankind into two classes, the owners of means of production and those who had only their labour power to sell, who stood in an increasingly antagonistic relation to each other.

By the beginning of the twentieth century, the trajectory of European (or western) societies had separated so considerably from those of other parts of the world that the particularity of 'Occidental rationalism', as Max Weber put it – not without hesitation – in the introduction to his comparative sociology of world religions (1920, now mostly read as the preface to *The Protestant Ethic*), had become a key topic of historico-sociological investigation (for a recent analysis, see Pomeranz 2000). The ambiguity of Weber's terminological choice has stayed with the debate on modernity ever since.

Weber seemed to claim both that rationalization had western origins and even preconditions in western cosmology *and* that it had 'universal significance', adding to the latter the much-overlooked parenthesis 'as we [presumably the westerners] are inclined to think'. Thus, it permitted both the promoters of later modernization theory and those more recent authors and advocates of the theorem of multiple modernities to refer to Weber as the main source of inspiration. The former, headed by Talcott Parsons, suggested that the western 'breakthrough' to modernity would (need to) be emulated by elites in other societies because of its normative and functional superiority, and that therefore western modernity would diffuse globally in processes of 'modernization and development', as the sociological jargon of the 1960s had it. The latter, inspired by the late Shmuel N. Eisenstadt, were not denying the 'universal significance' of western social transformations since the 1700s, but held that the encounter of other civilizations with western modernity did not lead to the mere diffusion of the western model but rather to the proliferation of varieties of modernity generated by the encounter of different 'cultural programmes', which had consolidated much earlier, with western ideas and practices.

The opposition between neo-modernization theory and the multiple modernities theorem, which marks current sociological debate on modernity, tends to sideline the third aspect of Weber's view of 'Occidental rationalism', namely a profound scepticism as to the fate of modernity. From this angle, Weber's reflections stand mid-stream in the tradition of a profound critique of modernity that was elaborated between the middle of the nineteenth and the middle of the twentieth century, with Karl Marx marking the beginning and Theodor W. Adorno the end, at least in its strong form, of this approach. Marx accepted the modern commitment to freedom and reason, as his expectation of a future 'free association of free human beings' demonstrates, but emphasized the impossibility of realizing it under conditions of class domination. Market liberty in bourgeois society would lead to alienation and commodification, human beings relating to each other as things. Similarly, Weber saw the Protestant Reformation as an increase of individual autonomy, eliminating the institutional mediation of the church between the believer and God (*The Protestant Ethic and the 'Spirit' of Capitalism*, 1904/5 and 1920). Once the social ethic associated with Protestantism, which emphasizes professional commitment and success, had contributed to bringing about the institutions of modern capitalism, however, a rationalized conduct of life would be imposed on the inhabitants of the 'dwellings made of steel' (the rendering of Weber's *stählernes Gehäuse* as 'iron cage' is rather misleading) characteristic of modernity. Adorno and Max Horkheimer (*Dialectics of Enlightenment*, 1944) provided the most extreme version of the theorem that the modern commitment to freedom and reason tends towards self-cancellation in its transformation into historically concrete social forms. They see the origins of this regression in the very philosophy of the Enlightenment that, in its insistence on the knowability of the world, transforms all qualities into mere quantities of the same and reduces the unknown to the status of a variable that is subject to the rules of mathematical equations. Such conceptualization entered into a totalizing alliance with industrial capitalism and produced, by the middle of the twentieth century, a society dominated by a culture industry in which nothing could be heard or touched that had not been heard or touched before. Novelty and creativity were equally eliminated in societies as otherwise different as the mass culture of the United States (the text was written in Los Angeles), Nazi Germany and the Stalinist Soviet Union.

Such radical critiques of modernity gradually lost their persuasive power during the second post-war period of the twentieth century. An echo of them is found in Herbert Marcuse's analysis of 'one-dimensional man' and 'one-dimensional society' (1964), a diagnosis the reception of which, in the student revolt of the late 1960s, both demonstrated its appeal and tended to undermine its validity since 'the cultural revolution of 1968' arguably (re)introduced a plurality of dimensions into the contemporary world. When Zygmunt Bauman revived the analysis of modernity as the obsessive attempt to create order and eliminate ambivalence (*Modernity and the Holocaust*, 1989; *Modernity and Ambivalence*, 1991), he did so partly in historical perspective, offering a novel view on the Nazi genocide of the European Jews as an utterly modern phenomenon, and partly situated his own writings at the exit of such organized modernity towards a postmodernity that reintroduced a concern with freedom, even though possibly a transformed and reduced one compared to earlier promises.

Such a view about modernity undergoing a major transformation had indeed arisen in the late 1970s, pioneered by Jean-François Lyotard's *Postmodern Condition* (1979). Lyotard radicalized the earlier sociological debate about a transformation from industrial to post-industrial society, promoted by authors such as Raymond Aron and Daniel Bell, by suggesting that the emerging social configuration was of such novelty that established concepts could no longer grasp it. Thus, his work contributed to launching a broad investigation, which has characterized much of political philosophy and comparative–historical sociology since, into the openness of the modern commitment to freedom and reason to a plurality of possibly interpretations. As a consequence, the earlier opposition between an affirmative view of modernity as the institutionalization of freedom and reason, on the one hand, and the critical analysis of the self-cancellation of the modern normative commitment, on the other, could now be reread as evidence of, first, the ambiguity of the conceptual underpinnings of modernity and, second, the variety of possible translations of those commitments into institutionalized social practices, such as democracy and capitalism (Wagner 2008).

This insight gave new impetus to research on modernity. In political philosophy and social theory, the nature of the ambiguity and thus plurality of the modern commitment required further investigation, not least with a view to understanding the degree of openness of this commitment to interpretation and to reviewing, not necessarily discarding, the universalist claims that had accompanied this commitment from its beginnings. In social research, the hypothesis of a recent major transformation of 'modern societies' between the 1960s and the present has informed many analyses from the mid-1980s onwards. Such research will need to address in particular the question whether such transformation, if it is ongoing, shows a specific direction breaking with or confirming the tendencies of modernity as they had been postulated in earlier theorizing. In the following, chapter 2 will address the question of the recent transformation of modernity and the plurality of modern forms from the angles of both political philosophy and social research. Chapter 3 will take up the question of the historical direction of the transformations of modernity and will review the concept of progress in this light. And chapter 4 will suggest a novel conceptualization of modernity that lends itself to the comparative analysis of contemporary societies and their historical trajectories, to be embarked on in Part II of this book.

Capitalism is the currently predominant mode of economic modernity, and it has been the central target of critical social theory since Marx. In turn, democracy is the dominant interpretation of political modernity, but it has been much less in the focus of social theory. Chapter 5 will ask whether capitalism and democracy are inextricably linked to each other, as much social theory has assumed, but it will renew this question in the light of the current debate about the unavoidability of neo-liberal capitalism and the prevailing image of incessant 'waves of democratization' across the globe. Chapter 6 will bring together the insights from the preceding chapters to explore the possibility of a comparative sociology of modernities, which will need to investigate whether (a) the observable *plurality of modern forms* of socio-political organization is (b) created from within specific *historical trajectories* and to explore (c) the *conditions for persistence* of such plurality under current conditions of globalization (Wagner 2011).

This threefold task is mindful of the interpretations given to Weber's reflections on modernity, but the current condition of global modernity tends to sharpen the issues raised in earlier theorizing. The plurality of modern forms may lend itself to varieties of world-making projects (Karagiannis and Wagner 2007), but at the same time the often observed homogenizing tendencies of globalization may impose a return to the view of modernity as a single and unique form of social and political organization that is without lasting alternatives. In that latter case, though, the critique of modernity may emerge in a new guise, as the critique of anomic individualization and reification that entails the risk of loss of world as a meaningful dwelling space, of worldlessness (see Arendt 1958 for the latter term; Honneth 2005 for the former). Chapter 7 will pursue this investigation further by focusing on one particular society and polity, South Africa, to understand how its historical trajectory was entangled with, but also differed from, the one of European modernity, if and how its post-apartheid modernity is specific in the current world context and, finally, how far we can learn from South Africa's modernity about the possible plurality of modern forms of life today. Chapter 8 returns from this case to the general agenda and will try to outline the contours of a world sociology of modernity that takes up the Weberian agenda in the light of the 'cultural problems' of today.

2

Changing Views of Modernity: From Convergence and Stability to Plurality and Transformations

A concept with a history

Has modernity always been or has it recently become a key concern in social and political theory? In the former view, social and political theory emerged in Europe in the aftermath of the great transformations at the end of the eighteenth and the beginning of the nineteenth centuries. The new social configuration that was forming as a result of the combined effect of the Industrial Revolution and the French Revolution demanded novel means of analysis and interpretation; and social theory, in particular (without that term yet being coined), was the new intellectual tool to grasp its own present time, that is, its modernity. Proponents of the latter view, in turn, point to the fact that the noun 'modernity' has come into widespread use in social and political theory only in the last three decades. A look at this recent development provides us with an angle from which to grasp the longer history and the transformations of the concern with modernity in social and political theory.

Just over thirty years ago, in 1979, as briefly mentioned earlier, the French philosopher Jean-François Lyotard published a short 'report on knowledge', which he had written at the request of the government of Quebec, under the title

The Postmodern Condition. Using data about the rapid diffusion of electronic information and communication technology, and building on earlier arguments about the rise of
'post-industrial society', he argued that modern societies
were undergoing a major social transformation and that
contemporary social theory was unable to grasp the nature
of that monumental change. He criticized both mainstream
social theorizing, epitomized by Parsonsian structural functionalism, and its critical alternative, as the exemplar for
which he referred to Jürgen Habermas's work, for operating
with reductionist and overly homogenizing concepts of the
social bond, and he maintained that contemporary society
was instead characterized by a multiplicity of social bonds
best captured by the Wittgensteinian idea of a plurality of
language games.

The little book contained provocative material for both
political philosophy and empirical social research that,
though much of it was not entirely new, had never appeared
in such a condensed form. It suggested that modernity was
neither functionally nor normatively superior to, or more
advanced than, earlier social configurations, as almost all
western social and political theory had maintained for one
and a half centuries. Furthermore, it denied the commonly
held view that modernity undergoes predominantly linear
evolution and reaches a stable state at full development.
Rather, it was about to undergo a radical social transformation that invalidated many of its promises of human emancipation. And the outcome of this transformation was the
coexistence of multiple forms of social bond in the shadow
of a diffuse concern with performativity.

In reaction to this provocation, two strands of debate
began to form in social and political theory during the 1980s.
On the one hand, the foundations of modern reasoning and
modern practices were reassessed in more philosophically
oriented debates, with Jürgen Habermas defending a sophisticated understanding of modernity in *The Philosophical
Discourse of Modernity* (1985) against critics such as
Lyotard, Michel Foucault and Jacques Derrida, and Richard

Rorty moving the pragmatist tradition close to the postmodern agenda in *Contingency, Irony, Solidarity* (1989). More sociologically oriented contributions focused on the question of the existence and nature of that new major social transformation that the theorem of postmodernity entailed. With *Risk Society* (1986), Ulrich Beck was among the first to distinguish a first and simple modernity, in his view rather well captured by sociological debate up to the 1970s, from 'another', 'reflexive' modernity that was about to emerge. In a whole array of writings published between 1987 and 1992, as mentioned earlier, Zygmunt Bauman forcefully distinguished between a modernity obsessed with the creation of order and the elimination of ambivalence from an emerging postmodernity more gently interpreting rather than legislating human relations (*Legislators and Interpreters*, 1987; *Modernity and the Holocaust*, 1989; *Modernity and Ambivalence*, 1991). From a focus on the critique of historical modernity, his more recent writings have turned towards critical assessments of the 'liquidity' of current social life (e.g., *Liquid Modernity*, 2000). Avoiding any strong notions of an epochal break, Alain Touraine (*Critique de la modernité*, 1992) suggested that modernity had always been characterized by the two tendencies towards subjectivation and rationalization, but concern with the former now re-emerged after a long period of predominance of the latter.

These were the debates in which the noun 'modernity' was introduced in social theory and political philosophy, which hitherto had been content with using terms such as 'modern society', 'industrial society' or 'capitalist society' for their main object. The purpose of investigation did not change with the terminology; the analysis of contemporary social configurations and the relations between the human beings that form them remained the major task. However, the change of terminology signalled that there was a need to reassure oneself about the nature of this object and about the purpose of one's investigations.

The doubts about the stability and superiority of western, 'modern society' were not confined to theoretical reflections during this period. Above, I briefly alluded to the radical transformation of modernity by comparing the situation in 1960 with the one of today. Now I can go into more detail and focus on the period between the late 1970s and the early 1980s as the years in which: the Iranian Revolution brought an end to the idea that non-western societies were just a bit behind on the same modernizing trajectory on which western ones had embarked, and Islamic world-views have since then increasingly been seen as challenging the prevalent western idea of modernity; the rise of the Japanese economy – and later the Taiwanese, the South Korean and now the Chinese one – suggested that a capitalism with a non-Protestant cultural background could compete successfully with the allegedly more advanced economies; the rise of neo-liberal ideologies (monetarism and supply-side economics as they were then known) to governing power in the UK, and the US, and the concomitant failure of Keynesian economic policy by a socialist-led government in France, signalled the end of the optimism that market economies could smoothly be steered by national governments. Furthermore, these years were bracketed by the student, worker and civil rights movements of the late 1960s that suddenly interrupted the tranquillity of the apparent post-war social consensus, on the one side, and by the collapse of Soviet-style socialism between 1989 and 1991, on the other side. There was plenty of everyday evidence at hand that suggested the need to interrogate anew the contemporary human condition.

Against this double background, the adoption of the term 'modernity' expressed the need for a new language for interpreting the contemporary socio-political condition, or at least the need for posing the question of whether a new language was required. The debate clearly drew on and referred to the long tradition of analysis of 'modern society', but aimed at reassessing that tradition in the light of new experiences that were increasingly being analysed as a profound transformation of modernity. In the remainder of this chapter, I will first briefly discuss that which is now the 'prehistory' of the modernity debate, that is, the social and political theory of modern and capitalist society in both its affirmative and its critical strands since the great social transformations of the late eighteenth and early nineteenth centuries. Building on the reflections in chapter 1, this historical look will facilitate the analysis of the outcome of the recent reassessment of modernity, which will be the second step, presented as the shift from an exclusively institutional to an interpretative analysis of modernity, which, more than the former, allows for plurality and transformability. Thirdly, this shift has given rise to a new opposition in most recent debate, which sees defenders of (neo-)modernization theory with persistent institutional emphasis reacting to the challenge from interpretative theorists of modernity who are now often lumped together by means of reference to 'multiple modernities', a term introduced by Shmuel N. Eisenstadt. This opposition, though, is rather unfruitful and the two subsequent chapters are meant to show ways in which it can be overcome.

Modernity as a set of institutions and its critique

From the early nineteenth century onwards, in works such as G. W. F. Hegel's *Elements of a Philosophy of Right* (1820), social theory and political philosophy worked on the assumption that contemporary western societies had emerged from earlier social configurations by way of a profound rupture. This rupture, although it could stretch over long periods and occurred in different societies at different points in time, regularly brought about a new set of institutions, most importantly a market-based economy, a democratic polity and autonomous knowledge-producing institutions developing empirical-analytical sciences. Once such 'modern society' was established, a superior form of social organization was thought to have been reached that contained all it needed to adapt successfully to changing circumstances.

However, a considerable tension between any historical description of a rupture and conceptual understandings of modernity comes immediately to the fore. The conceptual imagery of the institutions of 'modern society' sits in uneasy relation to historical dates. Were one to insist that the full set of those institutions needs to exist before a society can be called modern, socio-political modernity would be limited to a relatively small part of the globe during only a part of the twentieth century.

This tension between conceptuality and historicity was resolved by introducing an evolutionary logic into societal development. Based on the assumption of a societally effective voluntarism of human action, realms of social life were considered to have gradually separated from one another according to social functions. Religion, politics, the economy, the arts all emerged as separate spheres in a series of historical breaks – known as the scientific, industrial, democratic revolutions, etc. – that follows a logics of differentiation (Parsons 1964; Alexander 1978). A sequence of otherwise contingent ruptures can thus be read as a history of progress, and the era of modernity emerges by an unfolding from very incomplete beginnings. In this view, indeed, modern society came to full fruition only in the USA of the post-Second World War era, but 'modernization' processes were moving towards that *telos* for a long time, and continued to do so in other parts of the world.

In conceptual terms, this perspective on modern social life aimed at combining an emphasis on free human action with the achievement of greater mastery over the natural and social worlds. The differentiation of functions and their separate institutionalization was seen as both enhancing human freedom and increasing the range of action. Thus, the combination of freedom and reason, known from Enlightenment political philosophy, was transformed and, we may say, sociologized into terms such as subjectivity and rationality (e.g., Touraine 1992). Without this double concept being explicated in most of the theory of 'modern society', it nevertheless can be identified at the root of this conceptualization of modernity. At the same time, it certainly drew on what may be called the self-understanding of historical modernizers. Proponents of what came to be known as the scientific, industrial and democratic revolutions saw themselves acting in the name of freedom, and they also saw the new institutions they were calling for as providing greater benefits than the old ones.

After the dust of the great revolutions had settled, it became clear that the institutionalization of freedom and reason was a much less straightforward process than had been expected by Enlightenment optimists. As briefly mentioned at the outset, a series of major critical inquiries into the dynamics of modernity was elaborated successively from the middle of the nineteenth century up until the middle of the twentieth century. These critiques identified basic problems in the practices of modernity but did not abandon the commitment to modernity as a consequence. They all problematized, although in very different ways, the tension between the unleashing of the modern dynamics of freedom and rational mastery, on the one hand, and its, often unintended, collective outcome in the form of major societal institutions.

The first of these critiques was the *critique of political economy* as developed mainly by Karl Marx. In contrast to some of the conservative critics of capitalism, such as the German historical economists who flatly denounced its rationalist individualism, Marx basically adhered to the Enlightenment tradition of individual autonomy. His ideal was 'the free association of free human beings'. In the workings of the 'free' market in capitalism, however, he discovered a societal effect of human economic interaction that asserted itself 'behind the backs' of the actors. In an economy based on market exchange and forced sale of labour power, relations between human beings would turn into relations between things because they were mediated by commodities. Driven by laws of abstract value, markets would transform phenomena with a use value into commodities, the sole important criterion of which was the monetary value against which they could be exchanged. The result of such fetishization of products and money and of the reification of social relations would be the alienation of human beings from their work and its products, from other human beings and from themselves. In such an alienated condition, the possibility for autonomy and sovereignty of the economic actors would be completely eradicated, though these actors would indeed constantly reproduce these conditions by their own action.

The second grand critique was the *critique of large-scale organization and bureaucracy*, as analysed most prominently by Robert Michels and Max Weber. With a view to the enhancement of rational mastery of the world, it postulated the tendency for the formation of stratified bodies with hierarchical chains of command and generalized, abstract rules of action. In the context of a universal suffrage polity and welfare state, that is, in 'large' societies in which all individuals had to be included on a formal, i.e., legally equal, basis in all major regulations, such 'dwellings made of steel' had emerged as state apparatuses, big industrial enterprises and mass parties and would spread further in all realms of social life. While such institutions in fact enhanced the reach of human action generally, they limited it to the application of the rules inside the dwellings, so to speak, at the same time.

In these terms, a variant of a critique of conceptions of rationality is the *critique of modern philosophy and science*, the third grand critique. Weber, too, was aware of the great loss that the 'disenchantment of the world' through rational domination entailed. Still, he understood his own social science in rational and value-neutral terms, as he thought no other approach could prevail under conditions of modernity. In contrast, radical and explicit critiques of science were put forward by others in very different forms. The elaboration of a non-scientistic approach to science was attempted in idealist *Lebensphilosophie* and, in a different way, in early twentieth-century 'western' Marxism, i.e., by Theodor Adorno, Max Horkheimer and the early Frankfurt School. In some respects, pragmatism in the US can also be ranged under the critiques of science in as much as a new linkage of philosophy, anthropology and social science was proposed against the unfounded separation of spheres of knowledge in the disciplinary sciences. Such linkage would also bring the sciences back to a concern for the fundamental issues of the contemporary social world.

It was in pragmatism in particular – and in Europe in Durkheim's social theory – that a link between moral philosophy, social science and politics was maintained, or rather re-created with a view to responding to the contemporary problems of societal restructuring. This link gave rise to a fourth critique, the *critique of morality*. The problem may be schematically reconstructed as follows. The development of modern society entailed the risk of moral impoverishment, mainly due to two phenomena. The inevitable decline of unquestioned faith eroded a source that could provide foundations for moral behaviour. And if recurring face-to-face interaction often is the basis for the solidarity-supporting insight in the human likeness of the other, such kind of interaction would be decreasingly relevant in mass societies integrated on the large scale of a nation. The two questions that arise are, first, how to ground ethics at all, when no foundational criteria are universally accepted, and, second, how to develop adequate standards for morality, when social relations are predominantly 'thin' and at the same time widely extended in space and time, that is, to relatively distant others (Boltanski 1993). The requirements for ethics have been raised, while the likelihood to agree on any ethics at all may have diminished, in such a view. Again, it is the achievement of reflexively questioning any imposed standards of morality that may subvert the possibility of any standard at all.

Synthetically, then, an argumentative figure emerged as follows. In the historical development of modernity as 'liberal' society, the self-produced emergence of overarching structures, such as capitalism and the market, organization and bureaucracy, modern philosophy and science, and the division of labour, is identified. These structures work on the individual subjects and their possibilities for self-realization – up to the threat of self-cancellation of modernity. The more generalized modern practices become, the more they themselves may undermine the realizability of modernity as a historical project.

Modernity as experience and as interpretation

The interpretations of modernity provided by these critiques identified the tension between the modern orientations towards autonomy and towards mastery. They tended to resolve this tension in a clear-cut but also rather one-sided way, namely as the institutionalization of autonomy inevitably leading to forms of mastery that would subject 'free' human beings. Alienation, atomization, commodification, bureaucratization and instrumental rationalization would assert themselves as absolutely dominant trends, leading to the emergence of 'one-dimensional man' and 'one-dimensional society' (Herbert Marcuse). While this interpretation had some persuasive power, in particular during the first two-thirds of the twentieth century, in its totalizing way of reasoning, it underestimated the persistence of the ambivalence of modernity and the possible resurgence of the quest for autonomy. Towards the end of the twentieth century, socio-theoretical diagnosis of the present indeed shifted back to an emphasis on individualization, rather than atomization, and reflexivity, rather than rationality (e.g., Anthony Giddens, Ulrich Beck, Alain Touraine).

Although such recent analyses of modernity tend to employ the terminology of a new era (in response to the challenge of 'postmodernity' as discussed at the outset), they indeed draw implicitly on a different concept of modernity altogether. A common view of the history of social life in Europe holds that a 'culture of modernity' spread gradually over the past five centuries. This 'is a culture which is individualist [...]: it prizes autonomy; it gives an important place to self-exploration; and its visions of the good life involve personal commitment' (Taylor 1989: 305). Such an emphasis on individuality and individualization is quite alien to the totalizing critiques of modernity but also to the more formalized 'modern' discourses of the individual as demonstrated by rational choice theory or liberal political philosophy. And in the affirmative social theory of Parsonsian inspiration, the individual exists and indeed fully emerges only in modern times, but at the same time s/he is well integrated into norm-bound social life and appears 'deviant' when s/he transgresses those norms.

In European intellectual and cultural history, there has long been very little connection between the views of modernity and its inhabitants that praise agency and creativity in human beings, on the one side, and those that see the individual human being as either integrated in or submerged by social forces and structures. Given their interest in institutions and their stability, political philosophy and social theory proceeded predominantly by presupposition and showed little interest in actual human beings, who tend to be taken into account only as disturbances the more they enter the public scene. In literature and the arts, in contrast, the experience of modernity was in the centre and, as experience, it concerned in the first place the singular human being and her/his creative potential (Berman 1982). Michel Foucault's lecture 'What is Enlightenment?' very succinctly distinguished between those two readings of modernity. Modernity, as an attitude and experience, demands the exploration of one's self, the task of separating out 'from the contingency that has made us what we are, the possibility of no longer being, doing, or thinking what we are, do or think' (Foucault 1984: 46). It is opposed to modernity as an epoch and set of institutions, which demands obedience to agreed-upon rules. At least in some writers, like Lyotard, the idea of postmodernity was inspired by such a return to what had been a modern self-understanding since at least the Enlightenment, and much less by the idea of a new era 'after' modernity.

Up to this point, we have identified a double opposition in the ways of theorizing modernity. First, those views that see modernity as the institutionalization of freedom and reason have been opposed by critics that see freedom being undermined by a legislating rationality. Second, both of these views have been criticized for failing to take into account the actual human experiences of modernity and their variety. One of the outcomes of the post-1979 reassessment of modernity stems directly from the analysis of this constellation: if the opposition of affirmative and critical analysis of modernity persists over long periods without resolution, this suggests that modernity is open to a variety of interpretations. And if both approaches tended to neglect experience, then the elaboration of a more comprehensive interpretative approach to modernity should proceed by exploring the variety of experiences of modernity.

Such an interpretative analysis of modernity has gradually been developed over the past two decades, and it starts out from the proposed reference to autonomy and mastery that seems to mark, even though the terminology varies, a commonality across all theories of modernity and is thus a defining characteristic of modernity itself. Following Cornelius Castoriadis (1990; see also Arnason 1989; Wagner 1994, 2008), modernity can be considered as a situation in which the reference to autonomy and mastery provides for a double 'imaginary signification' of social life. By this term, Castoriadis refers to what more conventionally would be called a generally held belief or an 'interpretative pattern' (Arnason). More precisely, the two components of this signification are the idea of the autonomy of the human being as the knowing and acting subject, on the one hand, and, on the other, the idea of the rationality of the world, that is, its principled intelligibility. Conceptually, therefore, modernity refers to a situation in which human beings do not accept any external guarantors – that is, guarantors that they do not themselves posit – of their knowledge, of their political orders or of their ways of satisfying their material needs.

Earlier social and political theory also recognized the modern commitment to autonomy and mastery, but it thought to derive a particular institutional structure from this double imaginary signification. Thus, it was often inclined to consider a historically specific interpretation of a *problématique* as a general trait of modernity. This is the case, for instance, when the historical form of the European nation-state is conflated with the solution to, as it was often called, the problem of social order, which was expressed in the concept 'society' (Smelser 1997: ch. 3). When assuming, however, that a modern set of institutions can be derived from the imaginary signification of modernity, it is overlooked that the two elements of this signification are individually ambivalent and are between them tension-ridden. Therefore, the recent rethinking takes such tensions to open an interpretative space that is consistent with a variety of institutional forms. The relation between autonomy and mastery institutes an interpretative space that is to be specifically filled in each socio-historic situation through struggles over the situation-grounded appropriate meaning. Theoretically, at least, there is always a plurality and diversity of interpretations of this space.

An interim summary may be useful at this point. The social and political theory of contemporary western societies has long been based on the idea that those societies emerged through some rupture with the past. In this sense, scholars have long theorized 'modernity' as the attempt to grasp the specificity of the present, even though the term has been used only rather recently. The dominant strand has aimed at capturing this specificity by *structural-institutional analysis*. The modern institutions are here seen as the embodiments of the modern promise of freedom and reason. Against and beyond this dominant strand, three different conceptualizations of modernity have been proposed. First, the *critiques of modernity* have provided an alternative institutional analysis, emphasizing the undermining of the promise of autonomy in and through the workings of the modern institutions. Second, the *interpretative approach to modernity* has demonstrated the breadth of possible interpretations of what is commonly understood as the basic self-understanding, or imaginary signification, of modernity. Thirdly, the conception of *modernity as an ethos and an experience* has underlined the normative and agential features of modernity. In the former sense, it emphasizes the lack of any given foundations and the possibility to push the 'project of modernity' ever further. In the latter sense, it accentuates creativity and openness. In both ways, the experiential understanding complements the interpretative approach by underlining the large, potentially infinite, variety of interpretations of modernity.

Neo-modernization vs. the plurality of modernity

The theorem of multiple modernities, which has had the enormous merit of (re)introducing the idea of a possible plurality of modes of socio-political organization into the analysis of 'modern societies', did not emerge directly out of the theoretical debate as it was sketched above, but rather from concerns of comparative–historical macro-sociology, that is, the study of large-scale social configurations and their transformations over time. Within that field, though, it addressed directly the problem that had been inherited from the theories of modernization of broadly Parsonsian inspiration, namely the assumption of long-term convergence towards a single model of 'modern society'. Significantly, the approach that is central to this opening, pioneered by Shmuel Eisenstadt (see, e.g., 2002, 2003), explained the persistent plurality through 'cultural programmes', thus introducing an interpretative approach, in methodological terms, and some idea similar to the 'imaginary signification' of society, in substantive terms. This approach has been widely received and recognized (see, e.g., *Daedalus* 1998, 2000; some contributions to Hedström and Wittrock 2009); however, it has failed to make the strong innovative impact that one could have expected.

This – relative – failure is, among other reasons, due to two weaknesses of the multiple modernities approach: first, the strong idea of 'cultural programme' suggests considerable stability of any given form of modernity. Indeed, many contributors to the debate now reason in terms of civilizations, and 'classical' civilizations, like the Chinese, Japanese and the Indian ones, have been key objects for the identification of multiple modernities (see Arnason 2003 for the most nuanced contribution and chapter 4 below for further discussion). As a consequence, considerable limitations to the applicability of the approach are introduced, as it is difficult to conceive of South Africa, Brazil or even the USA or Australia in terms of deep-rooted, rather stable cultural programmes that merely unfold in the encounter with novel situations.

Second, the approach is based on only two main concepts: the characteristic (common and inevitable) features of modernity, on the one hand, and the (variety of) cultural programmes, on the other. This dichotomy limits the possibility of comparison since all difference between modernities needs to be explained in terms of the specific underlying programme.[1] In this light, either this approach does not move far away from standard institutional analysis that permits surface cultural variation in terms of mores and customs or, alternatively, any supposed incomparability across cultural programmes raises the spectre of normative relativism, a key concern of political theorizing committed to modernity (to be addressed below in chapter 3).

Indeed, the absence of a controversy between proponents of the multiple modernities concept and those who continue to work with a modernization approach – now sometimes

---

[1] The only exception is (north-west) European history, whose 'cultural programme' keeps being seen as having generated 'original' modernity, and thus the problematic primacy of Europe in the analysis of modernity is inadvertently reintroduced (for a discussion of the relation between 'civilization' and 'modernity', see Arnason 2003: 34–51). Ibrahim Kaya's (2004) concept of 'later modernities', developed in an analysis of Turkish society since the Kemalist Revolution, usefully points to a sense of crisis and need for change that may emerge in societies (or their elites) when comparing their own society with other ones that, for various and often partial reasons, are seen as superior or more advanced. Such an approach overcomes the conceptual dichotomy by empirically investigating the interpretative resources that are mobilized within a given society and partly retrieved from outside that society

referred to as neo-modernization to signal the reception of, and response to, earlier criticism – is striking. There is a profound opposition in at least two respects: the view of the dynamics of historical transformation, cultural resources on the one hand, a functional logic on the other; and the outcome of this dynamic, convergence towards a single institutional set-up on the one hand, persistent diversity on the other. Rather than giving rise to debate and exchange, though, this opposition seems to be seen as unresolvable by both sides and work concentrates on each side on the further elaboration of its own research programme.[2]

Both theoretical considerations and empirical findings have led the current author to side with an agency-oriented, interpretative understanding of modernity that makes the possible plurality of modern forms identifiable and analysable. At the same time, however, too many deficiencies exist in the multiple modernities approach and too many valid issues are raised by modernization-oriented scholars to make the avoidance of communication a viable strategy. The concept of modernity has rightly been criticized as often being both too comprehensive and too imprecise to allow operationalization for research and clarifying communication in scholarly exchange (see Yack 1997). Thus, a most fruitful next step should be the disentangling of the concept with a view to separating out researchable aspects of modernity that can be compared across the dividing lines of recent scholarship. Furthermore, such disentangling should be done with a view to making all contemporary societies amenable to analysis in terms of the specificities of their modernity (or lack of it) under current global conditions, not only either western societies or their counterparts in the classical civili-

---

[2] For rare explicit confrontations of the two approaches, see Schmidt 2010, heavily biased towards modernization theory though, and now Fourie (forthcoming), with observations on India; for an innovative comparative analysis of South and East Asian and South American modernities, indeed linking institutional with interpretative analysis, see Domingues (2012).

zations with their apparently stable cultural programmes. Such disentangling will be proposed in the remainder of the first part of this book across two steps. First, rather than assuming unilinear temporal direction of modernity, historical transformations need to be analysed in detail and the question posed whether the course of history is marked by progress (chapter 3). Secondly, a comparative sociology of modernity needs to be elaborated that analyses how economic, political and epistemic problems of socio-political organization are variably addressed in the light of modernity's 'imaginary signification' of autonomy and mastery in different parts of the world at different points in time (chapter 4). This comparative–historical approach will be applied to an exploration of the variety of present modernities and their historical trajectories in Part II of the book.

3

Successive Modernities: Crisis, Criticism and the Idea of Progress

Modernity has always been associated with progress. In everyday life, the belief – and commitment – that our children should have a better life than ourselves, expresses an idea of progress across time. As historians of concepts have shown, our idea of progress emerges in the late eighteenth century, and it gives rise to the view of a coming – bright – future that dissociates itself from the – often miserable – present. The horizon of expectations moves far beyond the space of experience, as Reinhart Koselleck (1979) famously put it.

The concept of progress is closely associated with that of revolution, which from the same time onwards takes on the meaning of an abrupt and radical forward step in time. The French Revolution was the first revolution of this kind, and many more socio-political events that we know under this term follow throughout the nineteenth and much of the twentieth centuries. Recently, however, the use of the term has become less frequent, and when used its meaning appears to have changed. The Iranian Revolution of 1979 is more often referred to as the overthrow of the Shah regime. And the collapse of Soviet-style socialism in 1989 has been called a 'catching-up' revolution by Jürgen Habermas (1990), awkwardly suggesting that socialist societies aspired to leap into the modern present rather than into any future. Such use moves the concept close to its pre-1789 meaning, namely, as an active socio-political transformation that re-establishes a good order – rather than creating anything new, it is oriented at a normatively superior past state of affairs.

Similarly, we seem to be losing the belief in progress. Realistic parents today – at least, but certainly not only, in the West[1] – know that it is unlikely that their children will have better and easier lives. Rather than openness of the horizon of time, uncertainty about the future prevails in a space and time in which youth unemployment is extremely high and life-courses are highly susceptible to future contingencies, in which technology failures cause unprecedented disasters and 'normal' technology application risks making the planet uninhabitable in a rather too well foreseeable future (on human-made climate change, see Chakrabarty 2009). Our present modernity may be radically different from the modernity of the 1960s also with regard to its expectations of the future, to its inclination – or not – towards producing normative superior futures, towards progress. This chapter will explore the relation between the analysis of modernity – its historical trajectories and current state – and the view of progress that we may hold in our time.

Increasing doubts: modernity and progress in historical perspective

In line with what has long been a widespread hope and belief, major strands of socio-political thought have assumed

[1] We will later embark more explicitly on comparative observations. Let it here be noted only that a major difference between expectations of the future may be related to the issue of whether a society can see itself plausibly as a creator of its own modernity or whether it sees itself as forced to respond to a modernity that unfolds outside of itself but exercises a strong impact. East European intellectuals, for instance, have tended to be more critical of modernity than West European ones (Arnason 2010); and the same experience emerges a fortiori in colonial situations (Ribeiro 1971 [1969]; Mbembe 2001).

that human societies pursue an evolutionary trajectory towards forms of organization that are in some way higher. In particular, it has been thought that the breakthrough towards 'modern society' in the course of the major social transformations of the late eighteenth and early nineteenth centuries marked the reaching of a superior state of history. The arguments varied. Political thought emphasized the commitment to individual autonomy and collective self-determination, to freedom and democracy. Social thought identified the functional differentiation of society that permitted better satisfaction of current needs and higher adaptability to future needs. Critical thought focused on flaws in the persisting class structure of modern society but held that just one more revolutionary transformation would eliminate this last deficiency.

In their strong versions, these interpretations of recent human history as the march of progress have lost credibility. Not everyone was inclined to accept Jean-François Lyotard's claim that the end of all narratives of emancipation had been reached because they had been refuted by historical events. However, the evolutionist theories were now recognized as relying too heavily on assumptions from the philosophy of history that could not in any way be 'tested' (using this term in a very broad sense) by historico-sociological research (see already Habermas 1981; and for a discussion Wagner 2001: ch. 5). In turn, the normative theories may in some way have established principles the validity of which one would not want to contest – the principles of freedom and equality being the prime examples. The questions, though, as to how far these principles have been realized in existing societies, and even if they have – importantly, whether the form of their realization leaves the guiding ideas of those principles intact – is often a matter of dispute.

Weaker versions of narratives of progress persist nevertheless. In sociological thought, simplistic theories of modernization prevailing during the 1950s and 1960s have largely been abandoned, but they have given way to neo-modernization theories that are less coherent but also more nuanced, the basic tenets of which are shared by many authors, even if sometimes implicitly. In normative political thought, few would deny that Jürgen Habermas makes a valid observation when he claims that the institutionalization of individual rights and of the rule of law marks an advance in human history, and even those critical theorists who raise objections would not discard the observation entirely but rather point to novel normative problems that arose in the aftermath and as a consequence of such institutionalization (see Karagiannis and Wagner 2008). The debate over the end of modernity and the rise of postmodernity during the 1980s and 1990s may not have had a clear conclusion, but by now one can see how the centre of discussion has shifted towards the exploration of forms of modernity rather than the end of it. Inadvertently (and sometimes one would want more explicitness), this means that the normative concerns of modernity, and similarly the questions where and how to identify their realization in the existing world, have remained significant.

In this new light, the idea of plural forms of modernity became the focus of attention. Sometimes it seems that this idea is by now widely accepted, but its implications are often unclear for a social theory and political philosophy that keeps normative concerns alive and aims to articulate them with socio-political analysis. It is often suspected that any embracing of the concept of plural modernities (under this or other names) necessarily entails the abandoning of normative concerns that ultimately are universal and unique, not plural and particular. In what follows, I will first briefly return to the 'multiple modernities' debate as it originated in Shmuel N. Eisenstadt's work, but now concentrate on the concerns about relativism that this approach has raised from the viewpoint of normative theorists, and will claim that these concerns – as is characteristic of debates over relativism – have not been conclusively addressed. Subsequently, I will shift terrain and discuss the plurality of modernity in analyses of transformations of modernity, 'successive modernities', as Johann Arnason called them.[2] Such historico-sociological analyses raise normative concerns about progress in a way that can possibly be more fruitfully addressed across the genre divide between historical sociology, on the one hand, and social and political theory, on the other, than in the idea of multiple modernities, since the point of reference is 'the same modernity' that transforms in time through the structuring activities of its own members.

The search for the dynamics of 'succession' under conditions of modernity leads to a reassessment of the notions of crisis and critique and the link between them and thus also to a reconnection between history and normative philosophy via a discussion of the meaning of 'critique'. Such reconnection then needs to be elaborated in more detail, and this will be done by using Axel Honneth's recent attempt at formulating a new, empirically rich and historically situated theory of justice as the theoretical object against the backdrop of which a reconsideration of the idea of progress can take place with the insights from comparative–historical sociology in hand. These reflections will engender further questions that will be addressed in the conclusion to the chapter: questions about material progress, about political progress and about the role of critique in current modernity.

Multiple modernities and the spectre of relativism

As discussed above (in chapter 2), the multiple modernities approach in its 'classic' version with a focus on civilizations

---

[2] The term 'successive modernities' was coined by Johann Arnason in his plenary lecture at the Congress of the International Institute of Sociology in Stockholm in 2005 and applied, among other authors, to my own work (Wagner 1994). This chapter is an attempt to spell out what such 'succession' means and I hope I can be forgiven for using the occasion partly for an exercise in reflection about my own prior work.

works with some assumption of 'original' diversity, which is postulated and then used to explain contemporary and persistent plurality of modern socio-political constellations. In normative terms, such conceptualization of diversity is highly troubling. Let us for a moment assume – knowing well that such an assumption has often been criticized – that western-style modernity embodies some normative principles, the adoption of which would mean progress. If so, which articulation of original cultural programmes would entail adoption of these principles and which would not? This question is in the background of topical debates about, for instance, the concept of human rights and its possible roots in religious traditions (see recently Stoeckl 2011), about the compatibility of 'Asian values' with the modern commitment to individual autonomy, about the possibilities of modernity in Islamic contexts, but also about 'multiculturalism' and its limits, an issue that currently haunts many European societies, but is addressed in much less sceptical ways in contemporary Latin America and South Africa, for instance. These questions are most often posed in Eurocentric ways because they assume that something that was crucial for the formation of modernity in Europe may be absent in other cultural contexts. But they are enabled by the assumption that the major world civilizations pursued historically parallel trajectories, without any significant exchange, until their encounter with European modernity. A revision of this assumption is crucial for the elaboration of a novel concept of modernity, and steps towards such revision will be taken in the following chapter, as well as throughout Part II of this book, arriving at a preliminary conclusion in chapter 8.

In turn, if we assume that the original cultural programmes embody normative principles of a potentially universalizable nature, what are the means to grasp what happens to them in the articulation with the arriving principles of western-style modernity? Theorists of multiple modernities, who work with this idea of parallel trajectories, normally do not claim that all modernities are equally modern. But they do not explore either along which normative lines modernities differ, thus leaving the question unasked as to whether the articulation of original cultural programmes with western-style modernity is – or can be – progress. That is why normative theorists often see the spectre of relativism lurking behind terms such as plurality or multiplicity when applied to modernity.

As long as the starting point of comparative analysis remains historical separateness and diversity, it will always be difficult to relate normative commitments generated within one context and identifiable there to normative commitments present in another context. One means to do so would be to use such universal commitments as a measuring rod, but that is not easily available. Philosophical debate has been, depending on what interpretation one prefers, either inconclusive in its work at discovering or creating universal normative claims or insufficiently concrete. In either case, the relation between an empirically identifiable normative claim and a universalizing formulation of an apparently similar claim may remain fuzzy.[3] Boaventura de Sousa Santos (2007: 16) recently proposed a 'diatopical hermeneutics' as a means of answering this question and tentatively applied it to exploring the relation between the *topoi* of human rights in western culture, *dharma* in Hindu culture and *umma* in Islamic culture. Such an approach is very close to the comparative–historical interpretative analysis of modernities proposed here and we will return to it later (chapter 8). At this point of our reasoning, though, we will not yet explore this issue further but just accept, for the purposes of this chapter, that the perplexities of normative theorists are understandable. The means to overcome them can more easily be created against the background of historico-sociological comparisons that do not start out from

---

[3] I am not suggesting that this is always the case. If the constitution of a state denies one group of its population the right to political participation, as under apartheid conditions in South Africa, the commitment to equality is violated. The introduction of equal suffrage thus can without doubt be considered as progress in normative terms.

separateness and diversity. The case of 'successive modernities' is the most clear-cut such comparison, a comparison
over time rather than across space.

Crises, critique and transformations of modernity

The theorem of successive modernities emerges from the
study of a particular kind of major social transformation,
namely that in which both the prior and the later state of
the transforming social configuration can adequately be analysed in terms of their modernity. This is a relatively novel
claim because the functionalist theory of modern society had
suggested that there would be no further major social transformation after a functionally differentiated institutional
setting had emerged. The only major transformation was
the one from 'traditional' to 'modern' society. Despite the
originally provocative nature of the claim to the contrary,
enhanced by a vocabulary that suggested overcoming or
superseding some features of modernity in the course of the
transformation (see above, chapter 2), the theorem of successive modernities is now widely accepted. It is applied,
even though often not with great clarity, in numerous sociological studies of contemporary societies and recent tendencies of change. Its dominant version employs the idea of a
transformation of modernity for a comparison of the current
state of society with its state prior to, roughly, the 1960s,
mostly assuming that this earlier state was well analysed by
sociological theorizing up to that point. This is the case, as
briefly discussed above, for Ulrich Beck's (1986) distinction
between a first, simple, and a second reflexive modernity,
which has also influenced Anthony Giddens's (1990, 1994)
considerations about institutional reflexivity as the novel
feature of modernity. A similar imagery occurs in Zygmunt
Bauman's (1987, 1989, 1991, 2000) writings about the legislating, order-producing, ambivalence-eliminating, solid features of (earlier) modernity that are contrasted with the
interpreting, liquefying characteristics of more recent (post)
modernity. Alain Touraine's (1992) distinction between the

subjectivizing and rationalizing features of modernity is more cautious in terms of periodization, but he, too, suggests that rationalization has long been the dominant aspect of existing modernity, more recently challenged by a newly rising concern with subjectivation. It should be noted that all these writings are underpinned by a normative agenda, but the evaluation of the two periods of modernity is, first, not the same across the authors and, second, not easily interpretable as progress or regress either. Rather, the authors point to new challenges created by the transformation of modernity.

These analyses work with an overly simplified picture of past modernity, taking the historicity of modern social configurations far too little into account. Aiming at more comparative–historical detail, my own reconstruction of the transforming modernities of West European national societies put a crisis and transformation of European modernities towards the end of the nineteenth century at the centre of attention, thus dividing the history of European modernities into three major periods rather than only two (Wagner 1994; see also Ewers and Nowotny 1986). Furthermore, inspired by Giddens's structuration theory, the analysis focused on the experiences of modernity by the social actors themselves and on the interpretations they gave to those experiences, rather than stipulating any actorless change in societal dynamics (as in Beck's case from functional differentiation to risky over-differentiation).

In this perspective, a social transformation is the outcome of a crisis of the earlier social configuration. Such crisis, in turn, is the perception of problems or shortcomings of the given practices in the light of principles, expectations or demands. The link between crisis and transformations is as follows (taking permission to quote myself):

> Practices have to be constantly reenacted to make them form institutions. If we see institutions as relatively stable sets of social conventions, then we may regard the building of such institutions as a process of conventionalization, and a crisis as

marked by tendencies towards de-conventionalization, followed by the creation of new sets of conventions. The chains of interaction that link human beings may be reoriented or extended and the kinds of linkages that are used may be altered, and so societies change their shape and extension. Crises will then be understood as periods when individuals and groups change their social practices to such an extent that major social institutions and, with them, the prevailing configuration of institutions undergo a transformation. (Wagner 1994: 31)

Such transformations are not directionless; one modernity does not succeed another one arbitrarily. Rather, a crisis of modernity is an event as a consequence of which societal developments are set on a different path (Wagner 1994: ch. 4). Despite the emphasis on individual and collective agency and problem-solving, though, normatively minded observers were not convinced that the opening of the analysis of modernity to the identification of a sequence of successive modernities would not neglect the whole question of modernity's normative commitments altogether (Habermas 1998).

This was a misunderstanding, but it was probably due to lack of explicitness in my *Sociology of Modernity* (1994), even though some 'logics' in the history of (western) modernity had been proposed. In brief: it was suggested that this modernity was originally built on highly liberal but socially severely restricted principles. The consequences of these two features were inequality, impoverishment and exclusion, and criticism directed against those consequences demanded inclusion, equality and social security. These demands were largely satisfied by the transformation to the inclusive, bounded and organized modernity that gradually came into being from the 1890s onwards and remained in place until the 1970s. But this transformation meant a strong standardization of practices and homogenization of life-courses, as well as the reinforcement of external boundaries. By the 1960s, the direction of social criticism in western societies had begun to change again, and the dismantling of the conventions of organized modernity meant extension of liberties and opening of boundaries (Wagner 1994: ch. 9). Luc Boltanski and Eve Chiapello (1999) developed a similar approach to analysing the transformations of French capitalism, which historically coincide roughly with the transformations of European modernity. They proposed the concepts of *critique sociale* and *critique artiste* to capture the different 'directions of criticism' and aimed to demonstrate how a particular capitalism is susceptible to provoking a particular critique and is then likely to transform in response to that critique (we will return to Boltanski's notion of critique below).

Later work of my own analysed the French Revolution, the formation of the working class, the building of welfare institutions and the adoption of Keynesian demand management as partial transformations of European societies by means of reinterpretation of existing views of society, polity and economy in the face of situations regarded as problematic and in need of collective action (Wagner 2008: ch. 13). Another study read the history of European political philosophy from the idea of state sovereignty to totalitarianism in parallel with the history of European political modernity. It suggested that principles of political philosophy were created in response to problematic situations and were then available for use in later situations. Those later situations could differ significantly from the earlier ones, in which case conceptual amendment and further elaboration was required. Significantly, some problematic aspects of novel situations could be the consequence of the solutions adopted for earlier problems (Wagner 2008: ch. 10).

Intermediate observation on history and theory

Before these socio-historical analyses can be reread in terms of the idea of progress that they convey (or not), the question of the relevance of historical analysis for normative theory needs to be addressed briefly. Philosophers are notorious for their difficulty in dealing with empirical observations unless the latter are constructed by themselves as exemplary cases to make a theoretical argument. Thus, the often-heard argument, the empirical coexistence of a plurality of institutional arrangements that embody modern commitments, has no relevance for a discussion of the universal nature of some modern normative principles. The claim underpinning this argument, which I otherwise fail to understand, must be that universalist reasoning cannot make itself dependent on empirical observation because it risks succumbing to particularity, that is, it risks falsification by reference to contradictory empirical evidence. In other words, universalist claims need to emerge from reasoning alone.

In my view, this position is untenable for three reasons. First, words are potentially meaningless outside of a context of application. Even abstract reasoning is abstracted from something, and while it may have internal linguistic coherence, cases of dispute will often need to be settled by returning to the concreteness from which they had been abstracted. Secondly, all our politico-philosophical concepts have a context of origins, which can often even be uncovered and explored. Thus, they are historical. They can be moved far away from their origins, or they can be stretched to cover large 'spatio-temporal envelopes' (Bruno Latour), but they remain historical nevertheless. Thirdly, validity is not necessarily affected by the inescapably historical, contextual nature of concepts. In particular, the history of modernity can be considered as a history of stretching concepts to cover the entire globe. This may often have first occurred as a mere claim to validity, but some concepts, or some interpretations of some concepts, have indeed travelled far also in the sense of having been accepted as valid. Philosophical believers in universalism and progress should also believe in the possibility of human learning. Thus, the expansion of concepts to cover larger situations, and be considered valid for them by more people, can be one indicator – not the only one, though – for their general validity.

There is no need to make strong general claims here about the relation between history and theory. All that was needed was to preclude the objection that nothing can be gained for normative considerations from empirical comparative–historical sociology. History and theory do not dwell in different worlds.

Historical sociology and social and political theory (1): critique and the generation of progress

In this sense, returning to the main thread of reasoning, the critique that is at work in transforming modernity is always of a theoretical nature. Its immediate cause is a social situation seen as problematic. The problem, though, is rarely of an absolute nature. It becomes a problem when judged by a standard that is, on the one hand, available to the actors involved but, on the other, external to the situation itself, and thus usable as a tool to measure the deficiency in the given situation (see Boltanski and Thévenot 1991). More particularly, in all cases analysed in my own prior work, which focused on Europe, virtually all such criteria of judgement stem from the era of Enlightenment and Revolution. They often refer directly to the commitment to liberty and equality, and on other occasions in more complex ways to reinterpretations of the commitment to fraternity, very soon to be rephrased as solidarity (see, e.g., Sewell 1980). For nineteenth-century actors, the double nature of these commitments does not seem to cause any concern. They are clearly historical, as they refer to a not-too-distant historical experience. At the same time, they already have a history of rapid diffusion and are thus endowed with general, potentially universal, significance.

Social change occurs in response to the critique and with a view to solving the problem. Often, it is innovative, it creates novelty, even unprecedented novelty. The possible consequences of the novel solution thus cannot entirely be predicted. Two examples from the history of European modernity may illustrate the issue: first, the French Revolution inaugurated the new political form of the republic based on popular sovereignty. Revolutionary optimists assumed that republicanism would spread quickly so that there would be no problem in building republics from the collective will of Europeans. Supportive but more sceptical observers (often German-speaking), in turn, suggested that some commonality of values and beliefs among the members of a collectivity committed to self-determination is required to make a republic viable, and the best evidence for such commonality would be the speaking of a common language. Such cultural-linguistic theory of the modern polity became the basis of national liberation movements, later nationalism and of the nation-state's policies of cultural homogenization. The theoretical argument is not flawed and not anti-modern either: it is committed to collective autonomy and defines the autonomous collectivity with a certain specificity. However, its proponents ignored or underestimated its possible negative consequences: that nationalism could become aggressive in a situation of competition between imperial states and economies; and that cultural homogenization policies could turn into both restrictions of individual autonomy and forms of exclusion.

Secondly, the liberation of market forces by granting commercial freedom, including the freedom to sell and buy labour power, was based on a whole series of normative arguments. The expansion of commerce would enhance domestic and international peace because of the mutual dependence on other human beings as producers of needed goods (the *doux commerce* argument). Specialization that results from production for a market rather than for one's own use would enhance productivity and thus increase the wealth of nations (the 'invisible hand' argument; see Hirschman 1977 for both arguments). And commercial freedom means the end of serfdom and of unjustified state imposition and is, therefore, itself a key expression of the modern commitment to individual autonomy. All of these arguments retain some validity. However, the experience of the application of such reasoning in the market revolution of the nineteenth century was impoverishment, rising inequality, and decreasing quality of living and working conditions, and a whole series of collectivizing innovations were made to counteract the effects of the individualizing revolution towards economic modernity: recognition of trade unions, collective labour law, social-policy institutions, protective barriers to trade, etc. (Polanyi 1985 [1944] remains an impressive account).

These two examples may suffice for the moment to elaborate an interim conclusion: there has been progress in the history of (European) modernity in the sense that socio-political problems have been identified and solved by recourse to action in line with modern normative commitments. In a direct, short-term comparison between two historical moments, there is often little doubt about achieved progress. Furthermore, such progress is not necessarily confined to short-term consequences. The end of serfdom and the introduction of freedom of commerce seemed so clearly demanded by the commitment to individual autonomy that juridical change in their direction led to the institutionalization of these freedoms as a means to safeguard normative achievements for future times.[4] However, there is no guarantee of lasting, long-term progress as the – potentially negative, unforeseen and possibly unforeseeable – future consequences of the problem-solving action may be larger than the current positive effect of problem-solving. From this insight from historico-sociological inquiry, we now turn to historically sensitive normative philosophy to see how the same issue is addressed from that angle.

Historical sociology and social and political theory (2): progress in historically sensitive philosophy

The normative political philosophy of modernity takes the dual principle of individual and collective autonomy as its starting point. There is some debate about the relation

---

[4] An early observer of modernity expressed caution with regard to the possibility of securing accomplishments for the future: 'Was Du geerbt von Deinen Vätern hast, erwirb es um es zu besitzen' (Johann Wolfgang Goethe, *Faust*).

between the two aspects of the principle of autonomy (see Wagner 2008: chs 2 and 3, for a critical discussion), but much of political theory considers this principle as a universalist accomplishment derived from the ideas of liberty and equality that are seen as following directly from the step of recognizing other human beings as equally human (the assumption of 'common humanity', in Boltanski and Thévenot's terms). Recently, the attempt at building a universalist political theory has been enriched by adding a theory of justice that is built on no other principles than the aforementioned but nevertheless succeeds in universally grounding some commitment to redistribution of resources, or solidarity (Rawls 1971). The main objective of this approach was indeed to separate the variety of 'comprehensive world-views' that members of modern societies may hold from the collective normative commitments of their polity, which can be honoured by procedural means alone. The modernity of given societies and polities could then be measured by means of this yardstick.

Such theorizing has been criticized for mistaking historical developments in some western societies for universal principles. In response, even defenders of the aforementioned principles have seen the need for 'historically situating' such an approach. This term has been used by Axel Honneth (2009) to refer to Habermas's analysis of contemporary modernity as grounded in the institutionalization of individual liberty through human rights and the rule of law in the liberal–democratic constitutional state. Honneth acknowledges Habermas's step towards historicization but criticizes the limitation to the liberal state as the sole institutional embodiment and defender of individual autonomy. In his view, elaborated at length in an earlier work (Honneth 1992), human beings need recognition not merely in the legal sense but also recognition for their contribution to the collectivity and recognition as a particular human being in private life. Thus, in addition to rights, human beings need love and respect.

For present purposes, Honneth's rich philosophy needs to be discussed only in two respects. In recent writings, first,

Honneth emphasizes that love and respect, like rights, are needed for human beings to live autonomously. Rather than considering recognition as itself a basic need, it is seen as a prerequisite for individual autonomy. With this step, Honneth aligns his philosophy with broader strands of theorizing and turns it more explicitly into a philosophy of modernity – for this reason it becomes highly suitable here for discussing findings of the comparative–historical sociology of modernity. Second, Honneth suggests that the pluralization of spheres of recognition requires a more nuanced way of historical reconstruction than the mere reference to institutional accomplishments in Habermas's 'historically situated proceduralism'.[5]

In Honneth's (2009) understanding, normative theory should no longer construct a neutral standpoint from which principles of justice can be identified and worked out, but rather reconstruct those principles from the historical processes of recognition in which they are always already effective as norms of mutual respect and consideration. Significantly, Honneth suggests that such theory can have 'confidence in historical reality' because the 'historically established relations of communication already contain', and 'socialised subjects are already guided by', the principles that the theory only has to explicate. This move is, on the one

---

[5] While I entirely agree with the step taken, the assessment of Habermas's work seems slightly unfair. After all, Habermas's most sociological theory of modernity, as contained in *Theory of Communicative Action*, combines institutional analysis (the distinction between systems and life-world and between economic and political-administrative systems) with reflections on social tendencies that upset or restore the balance between the spheres of society (the forms of colonization of the life-world and communicative action to rein in systemic overflow). Admittedly, there is little explicit history in Habermas's theory and he has not come back to it to, for instance, analyse commodification or juridification after the 1980s. But its explicit purpose was to assess progress and to criticize regress by means of substantive analyses of transformations of modernity, to use the language adopted in this chapter.

hand, an appropriate and necessary historicization of the debate about normative principles; on the other hand, it shows a fairly optimistic view of history and of the subjects and relations of communication.[6] Indeed, Honneth sees the need to immediately add an 'exception': 'where social relations are ethically entirely destroyed and demoralized, a reconstructive theory of justice becomes helpless' (2009: 17, my trans.).

The introduction of such an 'exception' provokes the question of how to identify normality. Or in broader terms, it suggests that even a reconstructive theory cannot entirely do without specifying basic criteria of normativity or, for that matter, without some concept of progress even after having abandoned the metaphysics of the philosophy of history – as Honneth (2004a) argues explicitly with regard to ways of interpreting Hegel's social theory. The utter absence of such criteria would then mark the exception; and, in turn, under conditions of normality these criteria can serve as a 'measure' (very broadly understood) of progress or regress.

In related writings, Honneth (in Fraser and Honneth 2003) has hinted at two such basic criteria, namely inclusion and individualization, with which the progress of recognition can be measured. The former seems rather straightforward. The more members of a given collectivity benefit from recognition, and the more they benefit from all forms of recognition, the more inclusive is this collectivity and, by implication, the more it lives up to normative principles. The latter criterion is more complex. At first sight, it seems evidently applicable: if recognition enables individual human beings to live autonomously, then higher degrees of individualization should signal a state of social relations in which

[6] Precisely, Honneth speaks about 'more confidence' than proceduralist theorists, who need a suprahistorical standpoint to arrive at normative principles. In another respect, Honneth is more sceptical than proceduralists because he sees the possibility that abstractly developed principles may place overly high demands on social relations.

recognition is widespread. However, the term 'individualization' is too ambiguous for such straightforward use. In the
history of social and political thought, it has certainly referred
to increasing possibilities of self-realization; however, it has
also been used for the uprooting of individuals from social
settings with anomie, alienation, conformism and related
phenomena as a consequence. As we shall see in conclusion,
both criteria reveal more of their complexities in historical
application.

Inclusion and individualization in European successive modernities

Have inclusion and individualization been the effects of
social transformations in nineteenth- and twentieth-century
(European) history? And if so, have these transformations
had a normatively desirable effect that outweighs their possible negative consequences?

As briefly alluded to above, inclusion has been a key
feature of European social transformations over the past two
centuries. By 1800, only male property-owning heads of
households were full citizens of modernity. Workers found
recognition as rights-holders and as contributors to the collective good through struggles from the 1830s to the 1970s.
Women found recognition as citizens between 1919 and the
end of the Second World War; they gained equal civil rights
to men often only as recently as the 1960s and 1970s; and
they have gained rights to their body through the legalization
of divorce and abortion that ended their being trapped by
legal force in unwanted private relations that often lacked
both love and respect. There has been progress through
inclusion.

However, two further observations complicate the picture.
The building of inclusive, organized modernity from the
late nineteenth century onwards was concomitant with
the raising of walls between national societies through
immigration restrictions, border controls, and so on (see
Noiriel 1991). Thus, processes of recognition inside national

boundaries went with external exclusion and, thus, denial of access to recognition. Arguably, the two processes are connected: the granting of political and social citizenship was seen as requiring a definition and delimitation of the citizenry. In other words, internal recognition may go along with denial of external recognition, raising the issue of justification of boundaries and of global justice and injustice. During the more recent transformation of organized modernity, in turn, novel forms of social exclusion (precarity) emerged after full juridical inclusion had been achieved and was maintained. There may thus be a connection between increased recognition of human beings as rights-holders, on the one hand, and, on the other hand, weakening of recognition of merit and solidarity – and maybe even of recognition in love and friendship when network capitalism erodes the boundary between work and private life (Boltanski and Chiapello 1999). Progress of inclusion in some respects has been accompanied by regress of inclusion in other respects.

Let us then turn to the question of individualization. The increase of individual autonomy has been a key commitment of European modernity from at least the sixteenth century onwards, even though it spread only gradually through society (Taylor 1989). From the early nineteenth century onwards, juridical change, such as the formalization of individual rights following the Declaration of the Rights of Man and of the Citizen and the granting of commercial freedom, gave a push to the orientation towards individual autonomy. Very soon, though, the negative consequences in terms of disembedding of human beings from their social contexts came to be felt. The subsequent long-term process of collectivization can only with difficulty be seen as further individualization. True, modern collective conventions and institutions include their members as individuals, but they do so by means of standardizing roles and homogenizing outlooks on the world. Tocqueville's insight that individualization may go along with increase in conformism was confirmed under organized modernity in the first half of the twentieth century, at that time often called mass society.

Unless we stretch the meaning of the term 'individualization' so far as to mean almost the opposite of what Honneth has in mind, the period between the 1890s and the 1950s can hardly be seen as having brought progress in individualization. In turn, though, the post-1970s individualization may go along with new forms of exclusion, as mentioned above (p. 41), and possibly also with new forms of anomie and alienation (as discussed, under the heading of 'reification', in Honneth 2005).

In sum, our brief application to the succession of modernities of criteria of progress as they emerge from normative philosophy tends to confirm the picture we have sketched above. We can identify historical progress in the transformations of modernity, and this should not come as a surprise as those transformations emerge from the articulation of critique and crisis in dealing with problematic developments within modernity. However, such progress in transformations does not constitute a long and linear line of normative improvement, as historical solutions to social problems may – and often do – cause novel normative deficiencies to emerge that are not necessarily of a minor nature compared to those that have been successfully overcome.[7]

Up to this point, we have provided an account of historical progress that employed two general criteria and applied them to the dynamics of social change over the past two centuries. Our observations had a focus on European

[7] This suggests a return to the question of the 'exception' of a totally demoralized society, for which Honneth has situations such as Nazi totalitarianism in mind. It is problematic, however, to tear such situations from their historical contexts. Nazism had its conditions of emergence in earlier German and European developments, and during its rise it was seen by many as a solution to problems of liberal restricted modernity. The radical decay of normative standards in historical reality cannot be dealt with by a change of approach and a sudden reliance on 'moral reasoning alone' (Hegel as referred to by Honneth) – or only at the cost of failing to understand the possibility of such decay and thus making its return more likely (see Lefort 1999).

societies, and this is a limitation we shall try to remedy in later chapters of this book (most explicitly from chapter 6 onwards). Even disregarding this limit, however, further questions remain that need to be addressed. First, our account neglected the idea of *material progress*, over which there may be less doubt than about the social progress explored above. Second, we touched only briefly upon what we may want to call *political progress*, namely an increase in the collective capacity to deal with problems – regardless of the substance of the problem at hand, which was in focus above. And finally, the *relation between crisis and criticism*, which we have sketched above as providing much of the dynamics of progress, may itself undergo historical change, not least as a result of the recent transformation of modernity.

Further questions (1): material progress

Some readers may have found that our preceding discussion missed the most important point: that modernity enhances the material well-being of human beings. Progress across the nineteenth and twentieth centuries in Europe and North America was most often related to an increase in wealth and improvement in living conditions, and these achievements in turn were seen as having been brought about by the application of technical advance in the original Industrial Revolution and its successors. Thus, the steam engine and the railways permit the exit from Malthusian law, allowing better provision of food for larger populations and avoiding the famines common in the past. Inventions in physics and chemistry are in the background of innovations in the electrical and chemical industries leading to life- and work-facilitating devices in the household and the firm and, thus, to the emergence of the consumer society, as well as establishing the preconditions for a new gender division of social labour. And most recently, innovations in information and communications technology have made the globe shrink and have given access to amenities ranging from unprecedented access to information to a new and more efficient global division of social labour. This is, in a common view, what modernity's attraction is really about. 'Later modernities', such as the East Asian ones, are successful precisely to the extent that they adopt western technical innovations, spread their benefits across their own societies, and acquire the capacity for further technical and material progress. In turn, 'alternative modernities', such as the Soviet one or several historical attempts in Latin America, ultimately failed because they proved unable to harness material progress in the same way as the West had done.

Some such view is at the centre of current neo-modernization theories, even though it is rarely made explicit there, and more obviously in much public debate. The striving for material progress needs to be seriously considered as an engine of social change, even though we will have reason to doubt the exclusive role of the West in pioneering this form of progress (see chapters 6 and 7 below). Importantly, such progress should not be measured in terms of economic growth rates, as much topical debate has it, but rather in terms of life expectancy, levels of health and overall living conditions. It would also need to consider variation within any given society, again not in the straight terms of social inequality measured by the Gini coefficient, but by inequality of living conditions and fulfilment of human needs.[8]

The view that modernity is centrally about material progress broadly understood, therefore, can be flatly rejected only at the expense of failing to understand a major dynamics of recent social change. Rather, one needs to integrate the above observations into the general analysis of the history of modernity. Three considerations are important in this respect.

First, the common view of modernity's material progress suggests that it is the result of the working of technical and industrial dynamics unleashed in European history,

---

[8] One may recall Johan Galtung's (1975) concept of 'structural violence' as the impediment to realizing life-chances that emerge from socio-structural positions. The Human Development Index developed by the United Nations now proposes a comprehensive statistical measure of progress along some such lines.

sometimes connected to the dynamics of market forces. We have reason to assume, though, that such dynamics on their own would have failed to bring about the advances in living conditions that Europe had reached by, say, 1913, had not other forces been at work. The 'social critique' at work from the middle of the nineteenth century, as discussed above, is more appropriately seen as the force that transforms a techno-economic potential into a broad societal benefit. And such force may accordingly be needed in the present and future as well to continue on the trajectory of material progress.

Returning to the concept of 'social critique', secondly, permits us to also evoke a first ambivalence in this kind of progress. The analysis of the transformations of capitalism elaborated by Luc Boltanski and Eve Chiapello (1999) suggests that progress in diminishing exploitation and oppression, in response to the social critique, may have historically gone along with increasing alienation, against which the 'artistic critique' should arise from the early twentieth century onwards. Thus, material progress is not without its own discontents, if not necessarily, then at least historically.

Thirdly, material progress has its 'side effects', its 'externalities', its 'unintended consequences', its *effets pervers* – to draw on different terminologies in economics and sociology for what are rather similar phenomena. Modern technology creates benefits but also hazards of various kinds, from pollution levels in industry and traffic to the risks associated with nuclear technology, most recently re-evoked by the Fukushima disaster in Japan. Even though these negative effects were never unknown, for a long time the debate about them was dominated by two convictions: that the benefits far outweigh the risks; and that the innovative human mind that created and applied these technologies would also come up with feasible solutions to reduce the negative effects or to keep them under control. The ecological debate that emerged in the 1960s strongly and increasingly challenged those convictions. Since the 1980s, human-made climate change and major nuclear accidents have become the key topics that changed the terms of the debate. In both cases, it is plausible to assume that the risks created are such that the inhabitability of the earth itself, or at least major regions of it, is at stake and that they are of such a long-term nature, with possible moments of irreversibility, that technological optimists would need to have even stronger confidence in the future human capacity and willingness to handle those risks.

In sum, the consideration of material progress adds a significant dimension to our view of modernity's inclination towards improving our lives, but it does not change the basic finding that any progress may entail regress that may be more significant than the gains achieved.

Further questions (2): political progress

The preceding discussion concluded with evoking a gamble on the future human capacity to handle problematic situations. Given the increasing dimension of some technologically induced problems, this is evermore a capacity to act collectively. The example of climate change, again, illustrates the issue. Proposals for dealing with the risk just in time are at hand, but their implementation requires global agreement and coordination, which at the current moment have not been reached. Thus, the risk of deteriorating living conditions, while being brought about by the side effects of technology and industry, may become actualized because of a lack of political progress, i.e., a lack of improvement in the capacity to deal collectively with problems.

This question opens up another dimension of the historical transformations of modernity. We can easily see that, hypothetically, enhanced inclusion and individualization, as well as material progress, might come about without enhanced capacity for collective agency. Many theories of social change have indeed been based on assumptions about trends or tendencies that are driven by some self-propelled dynamics without requiring human action and intentionality (for a critique see Boudon 1984: ch. 1). If we look in more detail at the historical sketch above, we recognize that the capacity for collective action changes in various ways across the trajectory of European modernity. The unleashing of market forces by granting commercial freedom can be interpreted as the renunciation of collectively organized production and distribution on the assumption that the aggregate of individual actions will provide a superior outcome. In contrast, the response to the problematic consequences of nineteenth-century capitalism and industrialism was seen to require an enhancement of collective agential capacity, both in terms of solidaristic social movements and in terms of the nation-state becoming more 'interventionist', as it was to be called later. Most recently, the debates over 'the decline of the nation-state' in the context of 'globalization' and 'deregulation' signal a decrease in collective agential capacity. Interestingly, looking at elite attitudes, this decrease has to some extent been a willed, or at the very least an accepted, one.[9]

This latter observation suggests that, indeed, a radical change in the prevailing attitude to political progress has occurred. From the early nineteenth century to the 1960s, intentional collective action was very frequently related to the idea that the world can be improved, that a better world can be brought about. Today, the experience that such action has often had negative effects is widespread in the West; and to engage in collective action towards truly normatively positive change is considered too complex and burdensome a matter to merit the effort (see, for a critique, Hirschman 1991, an argument to which we will return below, in chapter 7). As a consequence, there may be little of any concept of political progress left.

Accepting the challenge of this situation, Claus Offe (2010) recently addressed the question of which, if any,

---

[9] In subsequent chapters, we will first discuss this reorientation of the elites in the context of the 'legitimacy problems of late capitalism' (Habermas) in Europe (chapter 5) and will then show that it did not occur in the same form in other parts of the world (chapters 6 and 7).

concept of political progress is still sustainable today. His main conclusion is a rather sceptical one. Given the disillusion with past progressive efforts and the highly problematic current global condition – he mentions threats of war, energy scarcity and climate deterioration – the most we can realistically aim at is the avoidance of regress, rather than any political improvement at all. This appears like the epitome of a conservative credo, but it comes from a leading critical theorist. Offe looks here a bit like Edmund Burke (1993 [1790]) whose liberal beliefs were shaken when thinking about the possible consequences of the diffusion of the ideas of the French Revolution. But Offe writes more than two centuries after Burke, and this means after the experience of almost two centuries of progress-minded modernity. Rather than rejecting his reflections out of hand, we need to understand the angle from which he analyses the current condition of modernity.

In trying to do so, the notion of 'avoiding regress' is revealing. Rather than employing a straightforwardly conservative argument, Offe thus suggests that progress did occur historically. There have been normative accomplishments, upon which Offe touches in terms of lawfulness and institutionalized social solidarity. Both these terms stand in double opposition: lawfulness is opposed both to barbarism and to a blueprint of a model society; institutionalized solidarity both to poverty, hunger and social deprivation, on the one hand, and to redistribution, aiming at radical equality, on the other. The latter terms refer to the historical aims of progressive politics, the former to that which threatens if one does not aim today at avoiding regress.

In this more nuanced reading, we may appreciate Offe's concerns without fully accepting his conclusions. Globally speaking, there may well be need for further progress, and the slogan of the globalization-critical social movements, 'Another world is possible', suggests that progressive political imagination is still alive. Importantly, though, Offe points to the capacity for collective action, and indeed collective liberation and emancipation, as a key ingredient of the historical concept of political progress. His conclusions should be read as suggesting that the preservation – and we add: the enhancement – of this capacity is a precondition for reaching the substantive goals of avoiding future barbarisms.

Further questions (3): crisis without critique and progress?

Our reasoning thus far has underlined the following:

- that modernity is based on normative commitments that opened a horizon of expectations of better futures, of progress;
- that historical settings of modernity fall short of fulfilling the normative promises and thus enter into crises;
- that such crisis situations give rise to critique; that modernity undergoes transformations by addressing its problems in response to critique;
- that any such problem-solving may give rise to new, often unforeseen, problems;
- that the experience of several such transformations may cast doubt on the possibility of progress;
- that our current condition of modernity may be marked by a loss of belief in progress because the dangers created by modern practices outweigh any benefits one might expect from continuing similar practices.

This sequence begs one final further question: what about critique today? Continuing along the line of reasoning, one should expect a novel form of critique to emerge that addresses precisely the situation of exhaustion of the expectation of progress, despite the fact of considerable problems in the current condition of modernity. We have seen, however, that a leading critic withdraws from the tradition of critique. And even though Offe holds a particular view, disorientation about the currently needed form of critique, and its very possibility, is widespread. In conclusion of our exploration of modernity and progress, therefore, we shall address the transformations of critique in the history of social and political thought and explore the prospect of critique today.

Sociology has often been seen as a key component of the critical consciousness of modern society. Leading practitioners of the discipline, such as Raymond Boudon, Michael Burawoy and John Goldthorpe, have recently tried to reassess the task of sociology by distinguishing various types of practices and self-understanding, and, even though some of them have done so with a view to defending the professionalized discipline, none of them could avoid including an idea of sociology as critique in their typologies. This is due to the fact that sociology emerged as the discipline that studies the structure of social relations, and in particular the transformation of the structure of social relations, after the liberal–democratic and market-industrial revolutions that started in north-west Europe and North America in the late eighteenth century. Inspired by Enlightenment thought, these revolutions were undertaken in the name of liberty, but their outcomes were often seen as far from fulfilling the high expectations that had been raised. From their beginnings, sociology and social theory had a double agenda: they had to analyse the transformations of the social bonds in the wake of those revolutions; and they had to assess the falling-short of reality with regard to expectations. Thus, they were constitutively both empirical (and historical, as they were analysing social change) and critical. Whenever one part of the agenda was dropped, the whole endeavour immediately made little sense.

Historically, therefore, it seemed natural that the analyst would also be the critic of society, or more precisely of 'modernity', as the kind of society that emerged in the aftermath of the great revolutions. The scientific study of society would reveal insights into its failings that were not accessible to ordinary members of the same society. Karl Marx's critique of political economy inaugurated this conception of critique, as we have seen above (chapters 1 and 2), and in the German language it was further elaborated in the Critical

Theory (with capital initials) of the Frankfurt School, first in Max Horkheimer's programmatic writings and then in his and Theodor W. Adorno's *Dialectic of the Enlightenment* of 1944. In France, a somewhat parallel development can be discerned, leading from the emergence of the figure of the *intellectuel engagé* at the end of the nineteenth century to the embodiment of this attitude by Jean-Paul Sartre to, most recently, Pierre Bourdieu's critical sociology (for a discussion of forms of criticism, see Walzer 1988).

In the light of our reflections about the vanishing idea of progress, it is significant to observe that, in both the French and the German settings, a reappraisal of social criticism has recently been undertaken. In France, the starting point is Luc Boltanski and Laurent Thévenot's 'sociology of critical capacity' (1999), which locates the capacity for, and the practice of, criticism in the 'lay' members of society rather than in the detached theorist. Boltanski and Thévenot's work initially grew out of intense collaboration with Bourdieu during the 1960s and the 1970s. Since the publication of their *De la justification* (1991, in a first version 1987), however, their approach has increasingly been portrayed – and presented itself – as an alternative to Bourdieu's critical sociology, and the ties between what one may rightly call the two most important groups of social theorists and sociologists in France had been severed (for more detail on the approach, see Wagner 1999). Most recently, Luc Boltanski (2009) embarked on a reflexive exercise, trying to grasp the fundamental 'structure of critical theories' and then confronting in detail the sociology of critical capacity, or 'pragmatic sociology', of his own making with Bourdieu's critical sociology. His aim was to explore and explicate both the divide between the two approaches and their respective potentials for renewing critique under current socio-political conditions, which he refers to as 'democratic and capitalist societies'.

Boltanski's analysis was occasioned by the Adorno lectures which he gave in Frankfurt in November 2008, and thus by the encounter between the sociology of critical capacity and the recent research programme of the Frankfurt

Institute for Social Research, which is dedicated to exploring the 'paradoxes of capitalist modernization' and has been elaborated over the past years under the guidance of the institute's current director Axel Honneth. Like Boltanski's moral and political sociology, Honneth's social philosophy, as we have seen above, withdraws from the claim that the analyst has a superior critical insight into the workings of society and politics and aims at historically situating the normative claims against which social reality can be measured. Similarly, both authors and approaches do not wish to renounce the capacity for critique on the grounds of such situatedness and thus face the problem of justifying their critical leverage in the absence of strong epistemic claims – a task made more difficult by the fact that apparently more radical critiques, which had emerged from within their intellectual traditions, remain widespread in Europe and even gain persuasiveness in the context of the ongoing crises of capitalism and democracy. Boltanski's encounter with the Frankfurt debates thus provided material for a fascinating double comparison: between different versions of critique within intellectual traditions that have undergone transformations over time; and between two current research programmes that have renounced the grand claim of criticizing the contemporary social world from a higher standpoint but have turned to the critical capacity of the members of those societies themselves instead.

A brief look at Boltanski's reflections is useful before generalizing the argument. Boltanski is troubled by the possibility that the latter turn, towards 'lay' critical capacity, even though unavoidable and strongly promoted in his own works, spells the end to critique as sociology knew it. To regain a critical angle beyond the analysis of multifarious disputes and controversies which have been at the centre of the research programme in moral and political sociology that he co-initiated, he plausibly turns to institutions as social phenomena that, on the one hand, are created by social actors and can be changed by them but, on the other hand, always pre-exist any human being and appear to impose their rules on them. In the former sense, they are amenable to pragmatic sociology as the sedimented outcome of conflictual interactions; in the latter sense, they can be criticized by the detached analyst who focuses on their structures and the forms of social asymmetry and domination that they may entail.

At this point, Boltanski introduces a distinction between 'reality' as it is and 'world' as the repertoires of showing that every given 'reality' is always only one of a plurality of possible ones. As human beings are hermeneutic animals, they are always able, in principle, to relate to a given reality in such a way that a gap between reality and world may emerge. This is the space for critique – which is neither entirely beyond the experience of the ordinary members of a given society, as the earlier versions of critical theory maintained, nor limited to the encounter and interaction between a few members of that society, as it is in the nature of institutions to stretch rules so as to include larger numbers of human beings than those who actually interact. Precisely, Boltanski suggests, institutions tend to cover the totality of possible viewpoints of any experience and thus preclude plurality of interpretation. This is what earlier theorizing referred to as naturalization or reification. However, they are unlikely to fully preclude the interrogation of the 'reality of reality' because of the variety of human experience and the openness of their interpretation.

In more detail, Boltanski distinguishes three types of 'examinations' or 'tests' (*épreuves*) to which any given reality can be subjected. First, the test of truth is enacted in institutional practice itself to confirm existing rules and demonstrate their lasting character in routines of all kinds. The second and third types of examination, in contrast, are related to forms of critique. 'Reality tests' examine whether the practices of institutions indeed perform that which they claim to perform. As societies work with a plurality of registers of evaluation, as demonstrated in *De la justification* and later works of the Groupe de sociologie politique et morale in France, the possibility always exists that a practice may be ill-suited to the kind of test it is meant to perform and can be criticized on those grounds. Such critique is now called 'reformist'. Finally, 'existential tests' emerge from the experience of suffering, such as for reasons of injustice or humiliation, that are not (or not yet) in any way represented or representable – recognized, Axel Honneth would say – within the given institutional framework. The critique that emerges from such experience is 'radical'.

Boltanski's reflections achieve at least two important objectives. First, they support the notion that critique is an essential feature of the social sciences, in particular of sociology, and neither a residue of a pre-professional past nor an arbitrary addition by individual practitioners, because critique occurs in, and contributes to shaping, the social world that is being investigated. Second, they allow us to go beyond earlier forms of 'Critical Theory' and 'critical sociology' by situating critique as a social phenomenon in relation to a central concept such as 'institution'. At the same time, though, they fall short of reaching an additional objective that Boltanski also aims at, namely the use of his tools for the analysis of different societal situations and the possibility of critique within them, indeed with a view to a historical sociology the ultimate aim of which is to capture the specificity of the present – of our contemporary modernity, as we might say for our purposes. To reach this end, Boltanski's concept of critique is itself: (a) too 'presentist', not sufficiently rooted in a longer history; and it is (b) not situated within a broader, more comprehensive frame for the analysis of modernity.

(a) As briefly mentioned above, Boltanski's own earlier work, in particular *Le nouvel esprit du capitalisme*, co-authored with Eve Chiapello (1999), focused on the ways in which critique can provoke a crisis of existing social institutions and subsequently trigger major social transformations. His current reflections, though, do not return to the link between critique and crisis and fail to perceive the historical precursors and conditions. Most broadly,

Shmuel Eisenstadt's reworking of the 'axial-age hypothesis', the time-honoured idea of a major Eurasian period of politico-cultural transformation in the first millennium BCE, aimed at historically tracing the distinction between the existing world and other possible worlds and the dynamism that the existence of such a distinction potentially creates (see now Arnason, Eisenstadt and Wittrock 2005; and chapter 8 below). Closer to our own time, Reinhart Koselleck's analysis of socio-political change in the post-Enlightenment era, *Kritik und Krise* of 1959, at the outset of the author's important works on conceptual change, suggested a more specific recasting of the link between critique and crisis in the great revolutions of the late eighteenth and early nineteenth centuries and is arguably the first fully elaborated version of such an argument. In particular, his observation that the human 'horizon of expectations' gets detached from the 'space of experience' in which human beings live (Koselleck 1979) introduces in other words the distinction between 'reality' and possible 'worlds' that opens the space for critique for Boltanski.

(b) Whereas Koselleck's work provides a historical location for the debate about European modernity, Cornelius Castoriadis's analysis of the imaginary institution of society and the distinction between the instituting moment and the instituted one – mentioned only once by Boltanski – offers a conceptual foundation for distinguishing between different situations of modernity. Castoriadis insisted that our contemporary western societies, even though he called them 'liberal oligarchies' rather than democracies, were erected, at least partially, on the principle of autonomy. This principle has been weakened by the powerful presence of the capitalist drive to increase rational mastery (or pseudo-rational pseudo-mastery, as Castoriadis liked to say), but it has not withered away and remains present for reappropriation and critique of reality. Boltanski, in contrast, gives short shrift to political philosophy as 'the fiction that serves as foundation for the institutions' and does not – or hardly – consider the 'imperative for justification' (his words) that pervades our societies and institutions. Political philosophy, however, is better seen as a potential resource for critique, at the very least 'reformist critique', but in numerous current situations is also much more than that. Boltanski here seems to see 'fundamental democratization' (Karl Mannheim) as a rather irrelevant 'surface phenomenon' (Adorno in a review of Mannheim) and thus unfortunately contributes to the neglect of the political that marks much of critical theory, of both the Frankfurt and the Paris versions. In other words, he fails to see that institutions of modernity are, at least potentially, of a different kind from other institutions. They do not impose the 'reality of reality' but are based on the ever-possible contestation of their own contemporary, thus specific, foundations in the name of autonomy (see Kalyvas 2005; Karagiannis 2010).

It remains true, though, that the transformations of capitalism have engendered a reality that is undergoing constant change and in which such change is seen as both good and necessary, on the one hand, but appears driven by an impersonal logic, thus without recourse to autonomy, on the other. Hannah Arendt (1958) earlier referred to this phenomenon as the risk of 'worldlessness' and made it truly central to her own version of critique because human beings need to constitute a common world – not 'reality', as this is an act of language, of speaking together – that requires some stability as otherwise it could not be common. Such constitution of a common world has become ever more problematic due to the alliance of science and capital, as Boltanski rightly points out, referring also to recent sociology of scientific knowledge. It is also problematic, however, because it simply is difficult to reach strong substantive agreement between numerous actors who participate in deliberation on the basis of 'equal humanity' (see Wagner 2008: ch. 6 for more detail). Boltanski focuses, even though in different terms, on this risk of loss of world towards which a radical critique is in urgent need of elaboration. At this point, however, he seems to have somewhat lost sight of the need to constitute such critique in linguistic interactions between ordinary members of our societies on the basis of their experiences. He risks drifting back to the position of a critical theorist who stands remote from his contemporaries and has superior insight into the world.

To combat the risk of worldlessness, however, one needs rather to develop a world sociology of modernity as an intellectual tool that is based both on the critical interpretations that the current inhabitants of modernity give to their experiences and on the analysis of current global institutions as sedimentations of earlier interpretative and problem-solving actions. At this point, we have prepared the ground and need only to take one more step, namely the disentangling of the concept of modernity to bring the distinction between its political, economic and epistemic-critical aspects into view (chapter 4), before we can move on to analyses of transformations of modernity in more concrete terms, starting with a review of the relation between capitalism and democracy as 'critical', in the sense that democracy is the site from which critique of capitalism can persistently emerge and thus transformations of capitalist modernity be provoked (chapter 5).

4

Disentangling the Concept of Modernity: Time, Action and Problems to Be Solved

Up to this point, we have considered the recent transformations of modernity, the case for thinking about modernity in plural terms and the conditions for normative progress in modernity. As a by-product of our reasoning, we have entirely stopped referring to modernity, even implicitly, as necessarily a coherent social phenomenon and have focused on internal, possibly constitutive, tensions, on crisis, criticism and the possibly endless sequence of problem-solving and problem-generation instead. The next step is to take these latter insights to the comparative study of modernities and their historical trajectories to see in more detail how modernities differ and where they make progress, or not, in the realization of modernity's normative principles. This chapter aims to develop a conceptual and empirical programme to accomplish this task. To do so, it will first reconstruct the debate in social theory that accompanied the critique of modernization theory and its concept of 'modern society'. One consequence of this critique, as we shall see, was to question the existence of any collectivity that could be the 'unit of analysis' for the emergence of any form of 'modernity'. The concept of 'civilization', which we have already shown to problematically underlie the multiple modernities approach (in chapter 2 above), was proposed as a novel site for the analysis of modernities, but this proposal is not convincing.

The destructuring of social theory and the rise of civilizational analysis of modernities

Until the late 1960s, structuralism and structural-functionalism, and the accompanying sociological theory of modernization, had provided objectivist pictures of society that rested on the idea of strong ties between human beings guaranteeing coherence and a stable socio-political order. The conceptual elements varied between the approaches, but some combination of an interest-based, an identity-based and an institution-based explanation, emphasizing structure and social class, system and function, culture and nation, and procedure, law and state, respectively, was always at play. The analysis of entire socio-political configurations, then generally referred to as 'societies', did not appear to pose any major conceptual or empirical problem.

In the area of sociological theory, this thinking was challenged in all respects during the 1970s and 1980s. To give just some key examples: Anthony Giddens's work stands for the turn away from functionalism; Pierre Bourdieu's for the opening up of the structuralist tradition towards consideration of issues of temporality and agency; and Jürgen Habermas and Alain Touraine try to diagnose contemporary western societies without entirely fixing their institutional structures in any modernized version of a philosophy of history. In addition, empirical findings proliferated on subjects as diverse as personal identity and selfhood, forms of political participation or technologies and organizational forms of production, which all undermined the image of a generally stable and well-ordered society which had prevailed in the sociology of the 1950s and early 1960s. These theoretical and empirical developments have led to a situation in which many of the established categories of sociology have been challenged by a justified and irrefutable critique. In one sense, it seems as if contemporary modernity requires a new sociology for its analysis. In another sense, though, 'modernity' may itself look like one of those overly presupposition-rich concepts that can no longer be sustained, at least not as a term capturing the basic features of an entire social configuration (see Yack 1997).

In some strands of debate, the postulation of 'collective concepts' (Max Weber) without sufficient investigation of the social phenomena they refer to became the explicit target of criticism. This line of criticism recently ushered in an emphasis on ideas of increased 'individuality' and tendencies towards 'individualization' in contemporary social life. The emergence and assertion of the individual as a being without predetermined strong connections to or within collectivities has moved to the centre of sociological interest. Together with the parallel debate on 'globalization', a sociological image of the contemporary world has emerged in which there are no social phenomena 'between' the singular human being, on the one hand, and structures of global extension, on the other. The concomitant rise of an individualist-atomist ontology, most explicitly in rational-choice theories, makes it difficult to even conceive of social phenomena other than as aggregations of individual acts. The view of global-ization as an unstoppable and uncontrollable dynamics, as also largely seen in Anthony Giddens's (1990) metaphor of the 'juggernaut', underestimates the significance of its human-made character, thus its being amenable to reinterpretation and change. And the displacement of the idea of radical change from the collectivity and its history to the singular human being and her/his 'bare life' (Giorgio Agamben 1995) completes the new image of a world in which social relations may have global extensions, but are so thin and ephemeral that contemporary modern human beings are held to realize their own lives in a social context that they cannot conceive of as their own. As the earth becomes entirely subjected to human intervention, the world, in the sense of the social space that human beings inhabit, recedes into unrecogniz-ability – a situation Hannah Arendt had described as 'worldlessness', as mentioned above in the context of exploring possibilities of critique.

This is an image of contemporary modernity that at best captures some recent tendencies in the restructuring of social relations; it can hardly be upheld as the basis for a renewed sociology of contemporary social configurations. If it were valid as the characterization of inescapable trends, then the social world would become devoid of social structures as well as of forms of domination. It would be inhabited by individual human beings pursuing their lives by constantly reshaping their orientations, achieving what they achieve on the basis of their abilities alone, and moving in an open social space which itself would be constantly adjusting in line with the evolving orientations of the human beings that populate it.

This imagery does refer to observable transformations, but it conceptualizes them in such a way that their current force is exaggerated and their future continuation held to be inescapable. Importantly, the current image works with the extreme end-points of social life, the globe and the human body, and thus conceptualizes away any structured existence of 'the social'. Historically, sociology has always refused to accept any imagery of this kind. It has elaborated and insisted on an understanding of 'the social' as that which is between singular human beings, precedes their interpretations of the world and is amenable to reinterpretations. True, for some periods and for some authors, the concept of 'society' suggested that the 'social' had an eternal form – or had found its lasting form in 'modern society'. This was an error from which sociology has started to awaken. It now needs to take up its historical agenda of analysing and understanding the major transformations of the social, and it needs to do so with regard to the current such transformations, without accepting the ideological prejudice that those transformations spell the very end of this agenda.

In response to this challenge, some authors, and among them most notably and most subtly Johann Arnason, have revived the concept of 'civilization'. Noting the link between the concepts of civilization and culture, Arnason (2003: 1–2) neatly captures both the specificity of civilizational analysis and the two key dimensions any such analysis needs to address: 'interpretations of culture can focus on comprehensive forms of social life as well as on the constitutive patterns of meaning which make such forms durable and distinctive.' In other words, civilizational analysis deals with interpretations and meanings and it asks to what degree such interpretations are deeply *shared by a collectivity* so that they provide the basis of forms of life, and to what degree they are patterned so that they become *continuous over extended stretches of time*. Historically, civilizational analysis has mostly presupposed highly affirmative responses to both these questions of commonality and continuity. The current rereading in a pluralist light, such as Arnason's, turns such presuppositions into questions for analysis, even though arguably some considerable commonality and continuity needs to exist to speak of a civilization.

The following reflections are meant to explore how far such a concept of civilization can reach in analysing the contemporary global social constellation, or current global modernity. More specifically, these will raise some doubts about the ability of even pluralist civilizational analysis, and the associated multiple modernities approach, to fully open up to empirically observable lack of identity over time and a less than comprehensive grip of patterns of meaning on the members of a collectivity. The reasoning will proceed in two steps. First, a brief review of the recent conceptual debate in social theory and historical sociology will lead to the conclusion that concepts such as 'civilization' and 'modernity' often still work with too strong presuppositions about continuity and commonality and need disentangling. Second, a proposal will be made to distinguish several basic *problématiques* that all human collectivities need to address and to suggest that such a distinction lends itself to research-oriented disentangling of various aspects of social phenomena.

Continuity and commonality in the transformations of the social: from multiple modernities to societal self-understandings

The analysis proposed here engages with developments in social theory and historical macro-sociology such as: the return to human agency in the so-called 'structure–agency debate' of the 1980s (with Giddens 1984 as the main reference point here); the overcoming of evolutionist approaches and the critique of unfounded use of 'collective concepts' (Max Weber; most important here Mann 1993 [1986]); and the more recent elaboration of theories of social change that emphasize collective creativity and the reinterpretative, cultural component in every major social transformation (Sewell 2005).

Turning away from any idea of evolution as differentiation, theories of the constitution of societies see the formation of patterned social life not as the result of a meta-historical logic but as the work of human action and creativity. The terminology goes back to Anthony Giddens's groundbreaking volume *The Constitution of Society* (1984), which suggests a theory of 'structuration' of society that fully takes agentiality and historicity into account. Giddens offered a compelling critique of functionalism as a social theory that starts with a concept of 'society' and suggests a logic of evolution of societies in terms of functional differentiation but proves unsustainable on both theoretical and historical grounds. Alternatively, he suggested that any society is constituted through the practices of its living members who are, in principle, capable of altering through creative agency any 'social structure' that they inherited from the preceding generation. Proponents of differentiation theory, whether of a strictly functionalist or of a 'softer' kind, have never been able to respond convincingly to the critique by Giddens and other authors who participated in the return to agency in social theory. Giddens, unfortunately, never followed up on his own programme for a social theory of long-term transformations, but other, more historically inclined sociologists have taken up the issue and have tried to apply versions of structuration theory to the historical analysis of social configurations. For present purposes, the works by Michael Mann and William Sewell are particularly noteworthy.

In his *Sources of Social Power* (2 vols, 1993 [1986]), Mann provides an impressive long-term analysis of power 'from its beginnings' to the early twentieth century. He proposes an approach focused on networks of variable forms of power that may have different spatial extensions and different durability and, accordingly, rejects any notion of 'society' because it makes too many presuppositions about the coherence of social practices. He addresses the specificity of Europe, a theme central to sociological debate at least since Weber, in terms of the emergence of a 'European dynamic' after the crowning of Charlemagne as Emperor by the Pope in 800 CE. Significantly, Mann sees this event as a rupture that creates a novel trajectory, thus ruling out all possibility of considering the Roman Republic and Empire as the 'seedbed' (Talcott Parsons) of European modernity.

Mann offers a concise and innovative general conceptual proposal and then 'applies' it in lengthy analyses of historical developments. William Sewell (2005), in contrast, focuses on a more fine-tuned conceptual elaboration that has evolved from selective historico-sociological analysis, in particular of the history of the French Revolution and its nineteenth-century aftermath. For instance, he analyses the interactions between the Parisian population, the National Assembly in Versailles and the French king in the days before and after 14 July 1789 to see how 'the French Revolution' was created from an open sequence of local actions and interpretations. We retain here specifically the notions of an 'event' as a structure-transforming occurrence and of 'collective creativity' as frequently a key ingredient that turns an occurrence into an event in the aforementioned sense.

The juxtaposition of Mann's and Sewell's works as cornerstones for rebuilding a historically sensitive social theory shows that considerable problems remain. Sewell acknowledges that his approach, as elaborated thus far, will tend to favour relatively small-scale occurrences whose larger and long-term implications can be convincingly shown, as his analysis of the storming of the Bastille demonstrates, but whose analysis does not yet amount to an investigation of long-term developments as such. Thus, his work does not enable us to answer the question whether a common pattern of meaning, which we could call 'European civilization', pre-existed the French Revolution and provided resources for its possibility. Nor can we conclude from his work that the structure-transforming event of the storming of the Bastille marks the birth of modernity as a rupture with any preceding comprehensive form of social life. For the analysis of such long-term trajectories, Sewell merely points to Mann's work as an example that such an extension of his own approach is possible. Looking at Mann from this angle, in turn, it becomes evident that the conceptually guided description of long-term developments tends to lead to an imagery of multi-faceted, entangled processes of network expansion and contraction in which it becomes difficult to answer sharply posed questions about continuities and commonalities.

The problem thus is: The most persuasive work at the interface of social theory and comparative–historical sociology gives us little leeway to answer the question of whether there is in human history such long-term continuity and large-scale commonality that suggests the use of the concept 'civilization'. Does this imply that we need to 'drop' the question, to use one of Richard Rorty's favourite metaphors (e.g., Rorty 1989), to consider it as one of the concerns of the philosophy of history that have now been overcome because we have no means of addressing them? The following considerations are motivated by the insight that such 'dropping' is no solution. Methodological obstacles need to be overcome wherever there is reason to assume that some commonality and continuity exist, however difficult it may be to trace them in detail. There just may sometimes be social phenomena of large size and relatively stable long-term duration about which one cannot easily say how they, or some of their features, persist across large spatio-temporal envelopes.

Towards this end, the elaboration of a concept of 'societal self-understanding' is proposed here. Such a concept permits us to distance ourselves both from the traditional view that 'social structures' directly determine human action and cause social change, on the one hand, and the more recently arising view that all social phenomena can be explained by means of the aggregation of the rational actions of individuals, on the other. The very usefulness of the concept of 'society' has been an issue of debate within sociology (from Alain Touraine to Michael Mann, most recently Outhwaite 2005). The criticism is based on grounds of both empirical observation and theoretical reasoning. On the one hand, recent social change is said to have led to the dissolution of the coherence of national societies in economic, cultural and political respects; on the other, theoretical reflection has tended to deny the validity of Durkheim's proposition to see 'society' as a reality *sui generis* above and beyond human motivations and actions.

Valid as both of these observations are, it remains nevertheless true that human beings have endowed themselves with the capacity to act collectively upon their ways of living together and that a purely juridico-political concept such as the state does not capture the manifold ways in which such action is possible. Rather than abandoning the concept of 'society', the task is to reconceptualize it beyond notions such as 'national character', 'people's spirit' or 'collective identity', the more time-honoured ones of which had already been effectively criticized by Max Weber (Wagner 2011). The concept of 'self-understanding' provides a more tenable underpinning of 'society'. Rather than on high commonality among its members or on socio-structural cohesion, it focuses on communication between human beings about the basic rules and resources they share, and on the sedimented results of such communication. As such, it draws on the idea of societal *mise en forme*, implicit in Tocqueville and actualized by Claude Lefort (1986), and relates to Cornelius Castoriadis's (1975; Arnason 1989) concept of 'imaginary signification of society', recently popularized by Charles Taylor (2005).

Against the background of the deficiencies of the multiple modernities debate (as sketched above in chapter 2) and by implication much of 'civilizational analysis', the requirements for innovation in the comparative sociology of contemporary societies and their historical trajectories stand out clearly: for most current cases, *first*, the self-understanding of societies has not been stable for centuries but has undergone significant transformations, often even and especially in the recent past. Thus, there is no underlying cultural programme but rather an ongoing process of – more or less collective – interpretation of one's situation in the light of crucial experiences made in earlier situations (see Wagner 1994 and chapter 3 above). *Second*, rather than separating 'culture' from the institutional girders of modernity, one needs to demonstrate if and how reinterpretations of a society's self-understanding have an impact on institutional change, or in other words, how cultural-interpretative transformations are related to socio-political transformations (Sewell 2005; see Raaflaub forthcoming for a similar analysis of the emergence of democracy in ancient Greece).

In some recent scholarship, these two steps have been taken. However, the impact of these innovations is still limited, mostly for two reasons: first, the identification both of societal self-understandings and of their articulation with institutional forms still poses problems for research, despite important steps towards operationalization of concepts (see the following section); and second, there are inherent difficulties of substantively rich – i.e., not merely indicator-based – comparisons of large societies with rather different historical trajectories (to be discussed in chapter 6 below).

The basic *problématiques* of human social life: towards a novel comparative sociology of trajectories of modernity

The main challenge for an interpretative-institutional comparative sociology is the analysis of societal self-understandings and their transformations in such a way that comparability between societies becomes possible. Self-understandings may – and will tend to – refer to aspects and events that are specific to a given society, such as the moment of foundation – e.g., the (contested) idea of the birth of the United States out of the spirit of Lockean individualism (Hartz 1955) – or a highly significant collective experience – e.g., the (recently debated) self-understanding of the Italian Republic in the light of the *Resistenza* against fascism and occupation. These notions, valid as they may (or may not) be, do not lend themselves directly to comparison with other societies, or if so only on far too general a level.

In response to such important objection, it is suggested to abstract from those identifiable self-understandings those elements that concern a *limited set of basic problématiques* that all human societies need to address. In earlier work, we proposed a set of questions: (a) as to what certain knowledge a societal self-understanding is seen to rest upon; (b) as to how to determine and organize the rules for the life in common; and (c) as to how to satisfy the basic material needs for societal reproduction; and we referred to these questions as the epistemic, the political and the economic *problématique* respectively (Wagner 2008; for a related attempt at disentangling, see Domingues 2006). To say that a society embraces a *modern* self-understanding, furthermore, implies that all these questions are truly open, that answers to them are not externally given but need to be found, and that, therefore, contestation of the validity of existing answers is always possible.

The distinction of these *problématiques* marks a *first step* towards the disentangling of societal features that can then be systematically compared. In brief, the fact that societies need to effectively address these *problématiques* by searching for their own answers is what is *common* among all 'modernities'; the fact that the questions are open to interpretation; that there is not any one answer that is clearly superior to all others (even though one answer can certainly be better than others and societies will search for the better ones and/ or those that are more appropriate to them; see above, chapter 3) and, thus, that several answers can legitimately and usefully be given constitutes the *possible plurality* of modernity.

In a *second step*, the *range of possible answers* can be further identified in a relatively general and abstract way by scrutinizing the history of epistemological, political and economic thought – even though one will need to be aware of the risk of Eurocentrism if such reconstruction stays close to the currently established canon. In a very synthetic way, the following key issues emerge.

The epistemic *problématique* interrogates first of all the degree of certainty of knowledge human beings can attain with regard to themselves, to their social life and to nature. Historically, revealed religion and positive science have been seen as providers of such certainty, but both of them have been cast into doubt. Translating this issue into sociopolitical matters, it further raises the question to what degree such knowledge can or should be used to determine sociopolitical issues. Given that answers to both of the preceding questions can be contested under conditions of modernity, thirdly, one needs to ask how far claims to certain knowledge – in comprehensive world-views – can be made collectively binding in any given society.

This last question directly links the epistemic to the political *problématique*. The central issue of the latter concerns the relation between those matters that should/need to be dealt with in common and those others that should/can be left to individual self-determination. Modernity's basic commitment to autonomy leaves the relation between individual autonomy (freedom from constraint, or freedom from domination) and collective autonomy (democracy) rather widely open to interpretation. As we have seen above (chapter 3), the period often referred to as 'liberal' in European intellectual and political history, the nineteenth century, was not a period in which practices of collective self-determination, of democracy, became very widespread. Despite occasional claims to the contrary, modern political theory has not provided a single and unique answer to the question about the relation between individual and collective autonomy; thus, there is a plurality of interpretations. More specifically, the political *problématique* also concerns the extension and mode of participation in political decision-making (the question of citizenship) as well as the mode of aggregation in the process of collective will formation (the question of representation).

At the centre of the economic *problématique* is the question as to how best to satisfy human material needs, and it can be alternatively answered in terms of productive efficiency or in terms of congruence with societal values and norms. Among the latter, the commitment to individual freedom may rank highly in which case freedom of commerce will be considered an, at least partially, appropriate institutional solution. Referring again to European history, it has been argued for both markets and industry that they enhance productivity as well as freedom, but again critical debate has cast considerable doubts about such claims. Certainly, at the very least, other values – including value-based responses to the epistemic or political *problématiques* – can complement, or compete with, the value of individual freedom, in which case other answers are required (the classic study is Polanyi 1985 [1944]; see now Joerges, Stråth and Wagner 2005).

In all its brevity, this account should have demonstrated:

- that there is a plurality of possible ways of responding to these basic *problématiques*, even under conditions of modernity (against a key assumption of much social and political theory culminating in the works of – as different as these authors are – Talcott Parsons, John Rawls and Jürgen Habermas);

- that, further to their internal openness to contestation and interpretation, the responses to these *problématiques* can be articulated in different ways;
- that the need to articulate individual and collective autonomy is a thread common to all *problématiques*, and it is central to the political one.

Based on such disentangling of the concept of 'modern societal self-understandings', it is also possible to operationalize the analysis of major societal transformations, that is, introduce a historical, dynamic perspective into the analysis of, indeed trajectories of, modernity. Such transformations, and this is the *third step* of operationalization, will now be identified in terms of changes in the responses given to a single *problématique* or in the articulation between *problématiques* or both. Given the increase in specificity, compared to the more general concept 'self-understanding', such changes can often also be directly related to institutional change, such as, for example, constitutional change in the relation between church and state, or the forms of embeddedness of market self-regulation.

In historical analysis, such transformations can be traced to 'events' (William Sewell) in which actors respond to experiences they have made through reinterpretation of their understandings of the basic *problématiques*. Often, such an event will be the experience of failure of an established response to one or more of those *problématiques*. The reinterpretation will aim at providing a superior answer through the mobilization of the available cultural resources. This mobilization entails collective creativity; thus there is no cultural or civilizational determination (even though there may be path-dependency). In turn, there is no guarantee of the lasting superiority of the new answer, as any new response may generate new fault lines; thus, any view of societal 'evolution' as necessarily entailing learning processes that lead to higher levels of human social organization is equally flawed (see above, chapter 3). I will now, in a first step, try to apply such disentangling of the concept of modernity to a reconsideration of the relation between capitalism and democracy in the history of (predominantly) European modernity, in terms of varying responses given to the economic and the political *problématique* of modernity (chapter 5). Subsequently, I will employ the same terminology to compare European and non-European modernities, focusing on Brazil and South Africa (chapters 6 and 7).

Part II

Analysing Contemporary Modernity

5

The Link Between Capitalism and Democracy Reconsidered

We have seen before that modernity has often been equated with the institutional form of democratic market societies, and we have critically discussed the identification of the general concept of modernity with any specific institutional structure (chapter 2). Current modernity, however, is sometimes seen as undermining the force of this criticism. The transformations of the past three decades, which we have described above as giving rise to the pluralization of modernity, have also seen the rise to new hegemony – or the return to hegemony – of market organization of the economy, on the one hand, and of 'democratization' of politics across the world. Neo-modernization theorists often start out from this observation: that there is no alternative to market society, or capitalism, and to democracy. Thus, the basic idea of linear evolution and convergence has recently acquired forceful new evidence, in their view.

On a closer look, though it does not yet entirely refute this insight, current modernity is ridden by deep tensions with regard to both its economic and its political organization. On the one side, the spread of marketization across numerous societies after the end of Soviet socialism, as well as the emergence of a more deeply interconnected liberal-global capitalism, are beyond doubt, but at the same time this capitalism is more crisis-ridden than its predecessor was during and since the Great Depression of 1929. On the other side, the phenomenon that political scientists call 'waves of democratization' does seem to have enormous force, having now apparently reached the societies of Northern Africa and the Middle East who were considered to be unlikely candidates for democracy by many colleagues from the same discipline of political science. Alexis de Tocqueville's *Democracy in America* of the 1830s seems as topical today as Karl Marx and Friedrich Engels's *Communist Manifesto* of 1848. However, we have also witnessed disaffection with existing democracy, at least in the West, as well as a declining effective capacity for collective self-determination, as the democratic nation-state loses regulatory power when economic and cultural relations more and more frequently cross its boundaries. This declining governmental capacity is indeed sometimes seen as the main cause of citizen disaffection, a link rather strongly evident in contemporary Europe.

In this light, we need to return to, while rephrasing, some questions that have accompanied the analysis of modernity for a long time without being resolved. Towards this end, we can now use the disentangling of the *problématiques* of modernity, as proposed in the preceding chapter, to discuss anew the relation of democracy to capitalism and the ways in which both can be considered as expressions of modernity. It seems relatively straightforward to assume that democracy is the prevalent political form of modernity because democracy means nothing else than collective self-determination, with particular regard for the setting of rules for the life in common. The comparative analysis of varieties of modernity, while important, can quite safely rest on this starting assumption, even though, as we will show, it needs to emphasize the range of varieties of democracy. It is somewhat less clear, though, that capitalism is the economic form of modernity. In as far as every modern self-understanding resorts to a concept of autonomy, some authors do hold that a market economy best expresses economic modernity because it emphasizes the individual choices of the economic agents. At least two qualifications need to be added, though. First, market economy is not synonymous with capitalism. The former may be conceived as production and exchange by small individual producers, whereas the latter cannot be imagined without wage labour, thus a fundamental distinction between those who sell labour power and those who produce and sell other commodities, as all theorists of capitalism from Marx, Weber and Polanyi to currently Hall and Soskice (2000) and Boltanski and Chiapello (1999) agree. Second, the interpretation of autonomy as the freedom of the producer in a self-regulating market economy presupposes a prior separation between autonomy in economic matters and in political ones, which leaves the latter, even though its task is the setting of rules for the life in common, with nothing to say about the relation between 'states and markets', as it is often put. Historically, though, this relation was – and it still is – a matter of considerable dispute. As a consequence of these two observations, we need to state that both wage-labour capitalism and the self-regulating market economy are specific and partial interpretations of economic modernity, instead of being synonymous with, or identical to, the latter. And this insight opens the way to interrogating anew the relation between capitalism and democracy as a contingent one (for more detail on the general issue, see Wagner 2008: ch. 6).

Why should there be a link between capitalism and democracy?

At first sight, there is no compelling reason to think that capitalism and democracy should necessarily coexist. We know about numerous situations in history where capitalism flourished under non-democractic conditions and, though maybe more rarely in recent times, when democracy flourished under non-capitalist conditions. And indeed, the argument has been made that we refer here to two historically separate phenomena that, even though their emergence roughly coincided in time, have different origins, different underlying principles and, thus, different historical trajectories. Modern capitalism, in this view, emerged in England as the result of the Industrial Revolution (and of the related class struggle, in some interpretations), whereas modern democracy originated in France as a key item on the agenda of the French Revolution (Meiksins Wood 1999; see also Meiksins Wood 1996).

After further reflection, however, this view is rather implausible. In historical terms, there is too much of a coincidence between the two great revolutionary transformations to hold that, despite some spatial divergence, they are entirely disconnected. Both share an intellectual background in general Enlightenment thought that had widely spread, variations notwithstanding, across all of West and Central Europe and beyond, and specifically in the rethinking of politics, economy and society that was a key part of the Enlightenment programme. In particular, there was intense intellectual exchange between Britain, both Scotland and England, and France.

If we prematurely discarded the idea of a connection between capitalism and democracy, furthermore, we would deprive ourselves of the means to understand and analyse the current global condition of modernity. We face again a co-occurrence that, even if we may have difficulties in explaining or – for that matter – accepting it, is likely to be more than a mere coincidence. On the one hand, as stated at the outset, we have witnessed since the 1970s what political scientists call successive waves of democracy, adding up to what appears an unstoppable process of 'democratization'. And this institutional change is accompanied by a similarly inescapable discourse on human rights and democracy. From the 1980s onwards, on the other hand, we also observe the global diffusion of capitalism, to which allegedly 'there is no alternative' and which in its neo-liberal version is more and more shaping social practices.

For these reasons, it is more useful to accept the assumption that there is some link between capitalism and democracy. Paraphrasing Jürgen Habermas on a different matter, one might assume that there is some 'co-originality' of capitalism and democracy – that is, these phenomena have co-emerged historically and since displayed somewhat parallel developments – but leave open for the moment the precise nature of the connection. In a first step, we will reconsider theories that indeed have assumed that there is a strong connection, and furthermore that there is a strong conceptual reason that sustains this connection. In a second step, we will briefly review the history of the relation between modern capitalism and modern democracy from their beginnings until the 1970s to refine the ideas about such a conceptual link. These two steps will allow an interim conclusion to understand the double crisis of the 1970s, of both capitalism and democracy, an understanding that clears the way for getting a grip on the current condition of global capitalism and the alleged global movement towards democratization.

Conceptual reflections: from determinism to structured contingency

The idea that there is a strong connection between capitalism and democracy has long existed and indeed accompanied the history of both phenomena. However, it has been held in two contrasting versions, namely the conviction that there is a natural link between capitalism and democracy, on the one hand, and the conviction that these two phenomena are naturally in tension with each other, on the other hand.

The former idea, most versions of which would indeed not refer to 'capitalism' but rather to 'market society', have their origins in the assumption that political liberalism, the normative political philosophy that supports liberal democracy, and economic liberalism, the normative theory that suggests the enhancement of the 'wealth of nations' if markets reign freely, are nothing but two sides of the same coin. Despite its specific origins in political theory, on the one hand, and political economy, on the other, the notion of such a harmonious connection between political and economic institutions entered forcefully also into comprehensive social theories of 'modern society'. The most explicit version of such a theory is Talcott Parsons's view of modern society as being functionally differentiated. The organization of markets, on the one hand, and politics and public administration, on the other, according to their own logics would lead to a performative superiority, and an increased capacity to adapt to novel circumstances, of any society that adopted such differentiation. Underlying such a view is the idea of freedom as the guiding normative principle of modern societies. The wholesale adoption of this principle, and its translation into institutions, makes these societies both normatively and functionally superior to all other societies in world history.

More recently, doubt has grown about the adequacy of such theorizing, even among its erstwhile supporters. In the early 1970s, concern had grown about the 'governability' of advanced democracies as a situation seemed to have been reached in which the unreserved commitment to democracy led to such demands on the part of the citizenry that the economy could no longer satisfy the requests, leading to discontent and protest, on the one hand, and to the economic problems that were then called 'stagflation', a coexistence of lagging growth with inflation, on the other (Crozier, Huntington and Watanuki 1975).

The opposite view, that capitalism and democracy are naturally in tension with each other, was held by critical theorists from Marx himself to the Frankfurt School of Theodor W. Adorno and Max Horkheimer to the neo-Marxists of the 1970s. Across all variations, those theories held that a capitalist economy formed the basic structure of western societies, whereas democracy was nothing but a 'surface phenomenon' (Adorno on Mannheim, as mentioned above, p. 62). Temporary coexistence was possible but, in moments of crisis, democracy would tend to be abandoned to safeguard the interests of capital. As Horkheimer famously said, whoever speaks about fascism cannot remain silent about capitalism. In stark contrast to liberalism, the underlying idea here is that capitalism is exploitative and alienating. Under conditions of true democracy, thus, it was likely to be overthrown by popular will – if such will could ever express itself fully.

This thinking, too, witnessed rising doubts within its own ranks – doubts that were in this case enhanced by the experience of longer time-spans during which capitalism did indeed coexist with democracy. Starting with Antonio Gramsci's inter-war reflections on the impregnation of state institutions with the logic of capitalism and thus the need for an extended 'war of position' against capitalism, instead of a short 'war of movement' with quick victory, much of the work in this strand of theorizing was concerned with explaining the persistence of capitalism under conditions of democracy, culminating in the connection between 'welfare state and mass loyalty' (Narr and Offe 1975), that is, the observation that part of the surplus value was distributed in the form of welfare securities in return for electoral loyalty to capitalist principles. True to its original mission, though, such thinking also needed to explore the limits of such a formula, which was found in the observation – parallel to the idea of 'governability crisis' – that such distributive politics had exhausted itself and that, in its absence, 'legitimacy problems of late capitalism' (Habermas 1973) would arise.

Both theories tend to derive necessary institutional consequences from underlying principles in far too determinist a manner. Those principles, though, are open to interpretation and compatible with a variety of institutional forms. This can easily be seen by considering the historical fact that – we return to our starting observation – for too long, capitalism has coexisted with non-democratic political conditions for the liberal theories to be easily accepted, and there has by now been too great a persistence of capitalism under democratic conditions, even in times of crisis for the welfare state, for the critical theories to remain persuasive. Thus, a more nuanced analysis is required, and I will propose in the following a brief sketch of a historical sociology of democracy and capitalism as a step towards that end.[1] The question will be approached in two ways, starting with capitalism's relation to forms of democracy and moving on, in a second step, to democracy's relation to forms of capitalism.

Historical reflections: forms of democracy and capitalism up to 1970

For modern capitalism to emerge in Europe, initially in Britain, at least three conditions seem to have been necessary: the granting or extension of commercial freedom that enabled or facilitated both the engagement in production or commerce by the employers and the sale of their labour power by the workers – this is the legal change often motivated by the 'arguments for capitalism' (Hirschman 1977) that we briefly discussed above (chapter 3); the invention and diffusion of technology, such that work increasingly came to mean the operation of machines rather than the manufacture of a product – the steam engine is the symbol of what became referred to as the Industrial Revolution; and a social situation that either required or incentivized people to sell their labour power instead of working for subsistence or creating their own employment – the enclosures in Britain are the most prominent example of the creation of such a situation. By the early nineteenth century, these conditions existed to a considerable extent in a large region of the north-west of Europe, the region of early European capitalism. Inclusive

---

[1] European history will be at the centre of the following observations, but this kind of analysis is extendable to a global history of democracy and capitalism, and some remarks on Latin America and South Africa will be made, to be elaborated on in more detail in chapters 6 and 7. A historical analysis of social transformations is required to capture the dynamics between socio-economic constellation and political form, which comparative case analysis is unlikely to grasp (for probably the most elaborate such analysis, see Rueschemeyer, Stephens and Stephens 1992).

democracy, based on the idea of popular sovereignty, though, did not exist in any part of Europe at that moment.

Between 1800 and the end of the First World War, therefore, capitalism flourished under conditions of extremely restricted democracy. Until what is now called the 'first wave of democratization' led to universal male suffrage in numerous countries and even to equal male and female suffrage in some countries, the political participation of the working class was highly limited, and female political participation even more so. European societies of the nineteenth century have often been called 'liberal' on grounds of some constitutional guarantees and the diffusion of a basic liberal imaginary, but they were hardly democratic.

From 1919 onwards, in contrast, fully inclusive democracies developed in highly organized form with mass parties, high levels of political mobilization, high electoral participation and mass unionization. It is indeed striking to see how a principle that had been enunciated more than a century earlier and whose application had increasingly, but in vain, been argued for by the excluded groups of the population, was suddenly applied in numerous countries within a very short period. However, the granting of (male) universal suffrage at the end of the First World War cannot easily be seen as a step in a linear sequence of waves of democratization.[2] Numerous democracies were overturned – or cancelled themselves out (Karagiannis 2010) – by the rise of authoritarian, in some cases totalitarian, regimes such as in Italy, Germany and Spain, and the acquiescence with such regime to forms in the run-up to and during the Second World War in Austria, Norway, Vichy France and less pronouncedly in

---

[2] The experience of war – in particular the First World War, but also the Second – is highly significant for the transformation of European societies that are discussed in this chapter. Intending to elaborate a more general reasoning about the connection between capitalism and democracy, though, I neglect the consequences of these experiences for present purposes (for more detail, see Wagner 1994; Didry and Wagner 1999).

other European countries. Thus, 'democratization' was followed quickly by a period during which democratic regimes were overthrown either in civil wars/military coups d'état or through mass parties that gained power in elections but abandoned democratic rule afterwards.

Democratic institutions were mostly re-established immediately after the Second World War. In many countries, they have remained stable since, even though military coups d'état abolished democracy again for some time in the countries of Southern Europe (in Greece, and in Spain and Portugal the authoritarian governments of mid-century were long-lasting) and South America, before a new wave of democratization signalled the re-establishment of democracy from the 1970s onwards. During this entire period, capitalism continued to exist, with or without democracy, except in the Soviet Union and, after the Second World War, the socialist countries of Eastern Europe and East Asia.

For modern democracy to emerge in Europe, the specification of conditions is less straightforward than for modern capitalism. The imaginary of inclusive democracy became available, in principle, with the concept of popular sovereignty. But the ambiguity of the term 'people', which could refer either to all adult residents or to the lower classes, remained. The French Revolution was the moment when the street action of the people of Paris was connected with the expression of the popular will (Sewell 2005) but the widespread worries about the outcome of the French Revolution led almost immediately to the abandonment of such connection, to re-emerge only at the end of the First World War.

Thus, between 1800 and the late nineteenth century (in some countries later, until the 1930s), regimes with low levels of participation but strong aristocratic and oligarchic features coexisted across Europe with the liberal capitalism that emerged from the First Industrial Revolution. Enterprises were personally owned; many early capitalists were both inventors and organizers of production, and not unusually saw their relation to the workers as analogous to the father of a family in relation to his children, the company being a large household. The spirit of capitalism resided in 'the bourgeois' and featured the social ethic of devotion to work as a calling, as described by Werner Sombart (1920) and Max Weber (1949 [1904]). The formation of working-class consciousness, from the 1830s onwards, challenged this interpretation, but remained a long time dominated.

Between 1890 and 1930, that is, during the period of the build-up to and advent of the 'first wave of democratization', a combination of technical, organizational and economic changes transformed capitalism: the Second Industrial Revolution, focused on electric and chemical engineering and pioneered in the US and Germany; the 'managerial revolution' (Alfred Chandler), separating ownership from management; the emergence of 'finance capital' (Rudolf Hilferding), linking productive to financial organizations; the recognition of unions and the introduction of collective conventions; the 'scientific organization of work' (F. W. Taylor); and, finally, the introduction of a new wage regime, gradually permitting workers to buy the products of their own work (Henry Ford). The sum of these changes has been described as the creation of a new accumulation regime (Aglietta 1979 [1976]) of a mass-production, mass-consumption economy increasingly being referred to as Fordist capitalism. This is the capitalism to which Max Weber referred as 'modern' and as the one in which the 'spirit' of an underlying professional ethic had already escaped from the cage. It is, I add here, the capitalism that accompanies inclusive, organized democracy, but also the one that sees the temporary abandonment of democracy in early and mid-twentieth century Europe.

From the late 1960s onwards, the existing democratic rules were increasingly contested and put under strain, leading to the diagnoses of 'governability crisis' and 'legitimacy problems' alluded to above. At the same time, Fordist capitalism entered into crisis, leading to what we now know as the neo-liberal calls for deregulation and, more critically, to the emergence of 'network capitalism' based on the 'third spirit' of capitalism (Castells 1996; Boltanski and Chiapello 1999). This transformation can be related to the diffusion of electronic information and communication technology, sometimes referred to as the Third Industrial Revolution. However, the transformation is also triggered by increasing dissatisfaction with and, possibly, the decreasing performance of Fordist capitalism.

Interim conclusion: the democratic crisis of capitalism

I interrupt this brief double sketch at around 1970 because I intend to use it for the elaboration of a more nuanced set of hypotheses about the connection between capitalism and democracy, which will serve for understanding the most recent transformations of capitalism and democracy and the politico-economic constellation of the present.

First, capitalism can exist without democracy. Much of the nineteenth-century experience and the – often prolonged – periods of authoritarianism in various guises in the twentieth century demonstrate this rather clearly. However, the long coexistence of capitalism and democracy in Europe after the Second World War has tended to make us forget this historical experience and has generated the abovementioned ideas about the necessary connection between the two phenomena. To understand the recent advent of democracy, it may be useful to recall insights from the history of social and political thought that are rarely made explicit.

Social theory and sociology were little concerned with democracy up to the early twentieth century. Scholars observed transformations of social relations that were captured by terms such as industrial society, working classes, capital and the like, but – with the notable exception of Tocqueville – seemed to have concluded with the critics of the French Revolution and the 'ruling classes' that changes in political form were undesirable and, in the critical view, unlikely to happen unless capitalism had been overthrown. As I have shown above in the brief review of the idea of critique (chapter 3), this attitude has a limiting impact on social theory that can still be felt today. This long neglect of the democratic possibilities of modernity ended only after the arrival of extended or universal (male) suffrage. From the late nineteenth century, Italian scholars focused in neo-Aristotelian or, as has more often been underlined, neo-Machiavellian fashion on the relation between the elite political class and the multitude. But only from 1919 onwards does democracy become a key concern of social and political thought, starting with Weber's last writings and leading to seminal works by authors such as Carl Schmitt, Joseph Schumpeter, Karl Mannheim, and in the US John Dewey as well as Antonio Gramsci – in some way also Rosa Luxemburg – among the few Marxists engaging this topic. Significantly, much of this thinking about democracy in the early twentieth century is very open and critical. Democracy is seen as a novel political form that is – or at least can be – highly problematic. It is only after the Second World War that the conviction that 'there is no alternative' to democracy becomes widespread.

Secondly, whenever capitalism exists without democracy, it will be exposed to a critique of exploitation and injustice, likely to be expressed through calls for inclusive, egalitarian democracy. If absence of democracy was characteristic of nineteenth-century capitalism, how should we understand the long dormancy of the democratic political imaginary and its breakthrough in the early twentieth century? Capitalism is a form of economic organization that is marked by two features that are crucial for answering our question. First, it purports to solve the question of the satisfaction of human material needs – the economic *problématique*, as detailed above (chapter 4) – by indirect means, by counting on the interest of the commodity producer in a context of production for markets. Second, it creates a distinction between a group of economic agents that decides about production and another one that is subject to the commands of the former group. These two features make it distinct from both the ancient economy, in which masters commanded slaves but production was directly oriented at satisfying needs, on the one hand, and from (market) socialism, in which everyone has a say in decisions over production, on the other. As a first consequence, a situation of lacking satisfaction of needs, given the capacity of the existing economy, becomes likely for three distinct reasons: deteriorating living and working conditions during the rise of capitalism and exit from the preceding form of economic organization; exploitation in the sense of appropriation of the major share of production by those who command production decisions; and crises of market self-regulation that entail production below the potential and/or destruction of products that cannot be sold. While such a situation of dissatisfaction, secondly, may in principle be addressed by a number of different remedies, an immediately plausible suggestion is that all those involved in, or affected by, the existing situation should participate equally in improving the situation. More briefly, if social problems persist in a context of domination and exclusion from participation, then equal collective self-determination – inclusive democracy – is a prima facie plausible and persuasive proposal for addressing these problems more satisfactorily.

Some qualified application of this reasoning, I suggest, goes quite far in explaining moves towards democracy under conditions of capitalism. This holds both for the 'original' and slow rise of democracy in nineteenth- and early twentieth-century Europe and for the end of the authoritarian regimes of the twentieth century. Similarly, one might consider the much-debated likelihood of the People's Republic of China's future move towards liberal democracy in this light, rather than applying some version of the simplistic argument of the necessary connection between market economy and democracy, between economic liberalism and political liberalism.

There is at least one further consideration to be made, though. The preceding reasoning may explain why the dominated classes call for democracy, but no reason has yet been provided for why the dominating classes should yield to this demand. To some extent, one may be able to count on the force of the argument – we will explicitly address the need for justification under conditions of modernity below (in chapter 7) – but such force alone is unlikely to always prevail. Historically, we can recognize that the dominant class in capitalism has in two main ways been dependent on the dominated class. First, industrial mass production relied on large numbers of workers who needed to some extent to be willing to work, given that this was 'free labour', even though Frederick W. Taylor tried to dissociate will and performance at the workplace and Max Weber maintained that modern capitalism did not require motivation any longer. Strikes have historically been effective because the withdrawal of the willingness to work touches capitalism at its core. Secondly, emerging mass-consumption capitalism required workers to buy the products of their own production, which in turn necessitates effective demand in the double sense of having the means to buy and being willing to buy the commodities offered. Fordist capitalism, in brief, was the historical outcome of the combined effect of the considerations above.

Thirdly, when capitalism coexists with inclusive democracy in bounded collectivities with strong internal social bonds, pressure on profitability can be high and lead to crises. The above reasoning, to turn it another way, suggests that the absence of inclusive democracy became a problem for nineteenth-century European capitalism and that the introduction of democracy helped to ease some of the pressure on this form of economic organization, in terms of both increasing legitimacy and solving profitability problems – counteracting the tendency of the rate of profit to fall, as Marx had put it, by creating a new accumulation regime. However, the new Fordist capitalism that acknowledged its need for support by the masses also created for itself a new set of problems, many of which were precisely problems with democracy.

We can distinguish two historical attempts at addressing this novel problem. First, the very introduction of inclusive democracy was fraught because of the dominant class's fear of an imminent socialist revolution, based on the observation that workers' parties and trade unions were pressing beyond the right to formal political participation for the creation of economic and social rights that would indeed have limited the power of the dominant class. The early thinking about modern democracy, alluded to above, is radical and critical in underlining the risks that democracy brings for the established socio-economic arrangement because those fears were well recognized. The anti-democratic turns of the early twentieth century that often entailed the temporary cancellation of the just-inaugurated democracies were the first solution to this problem.

Second, the re-establishment of democratic political arrangements after the Second World War occurred under different auspices, explained to a large extent by the experience of the class struggle, civil war and war that preceded it. In the most conflict-ridden countries, such as (West) Germany, for instance, most social and political groups adopted a moderate, accommodating stand towards the reconstitution of economic and political institutions, building what has become labelled a 'consociational democracy' in which rather different convictions and interests coexist by virtue of their not being entered into the common, collective arrangements (for the term, see Lijphart 1975). In parallel, the theorizing of democracy changed form. On the one hand, democracy now became central to political thought, leading post-Second World War political science to be considered as 'the science of democracy'. On the other hand, much of this thinking was concerned with limiting the political passions, suggesting, for instance, that a certain degree of citizens' apathy is a precondition for viable democracies (Almond and Verba 1963) or that organized representation will and should have the effect of filtering the more conflictive components of political debate so that they would not reach decision-making institutions (see Avritzer 2007 for a highly instructive account).

Whereas the first experience suggested that democracy may be incompatible with capitalism, the second attempt was marked by the effort to demonstrate that democracy and capitalism were compatible – drawing conclusions also from the experiences of some Scandinavian countries and the United Kingdom, as well as the United States, where this seemed to have been the case. By the late 1960s, however, this attempt appeared to have reached its limits.

Fourthly, the rise of what has become known as neo-liberal global capitalism can, to a considerable extent, be understood as the outcome of a democratic crisis of capitalism. At this point, we return to our opening observation (see chapter 2) that the decade from the late 1960s to the late 1970s witnessed a large number of apparently disconnected events that in their sum suggested that, contrary to all prior assumptions, modernity had started to undergo a major social transformation. In brief, these events are:

- the students' revolt of 1968;
- the return of spontaneous and large-scale working-class action in 1968 and 1969;
- the end of the international monetary system as established in Bretton Woods;
- the defeat of the US armed forces in the Vietnam War;
- the first general recession of the so-called advanced industrial economies since the end of the Second World War in 1974/5 and the rising doubts about the effectiveness of Keynesian demand management;
- the rise of the Japanese economy to world-market competitiveness;
- the oil price crises in 1973 and 1979;
- the Iranian Revolution in 1979; and
- the election of Margaret Thatcher in 1979 and Ronald Reagan in 1980 to government power in the UK and the US with neo-liberal, anti-union economic policies.

In terms of the sequence of events and action, this period can rather neatly be described as the move from the expression of a crisis through the workers' (and students') demands, the impossibility of resolving it through the established instruments such as concerted action between employers, governments and unions and Keynesianism, the deepening of the crisis through seemingly external events in East Asia and the Middle East, the increasing reception of more radical measures, such as monetarism and supply-side economics in economic policy thinking, and finally the adoption of such measures in government policies. In more substantive terms, we witness the rise of democratic pressures on profitability, recognized also by critical scholars (Glyn and Sutcliffe 1972), because of dissatisfaction with working and living conditions, now seen more as alienating than as exploitative (Boltanski and Chiapello 1999). But the outcome now was neither the creation of socialism, as hoped or feared in 1919, nor the abolition of democracy, as performed in the 1920s and 1930s, but the deflection of the critical concerns in a transformation of both capitalism and democracy.

In other words, the 'governability crisis' and the 'legitimacy problems of late capitalism' did exist but they were resolved by the early 1970s in a way that was rather unexpected. The processes we now refer summarily to as 'economic globalization', namely neo-liberalism, deregulation, structural adjustment and shock therapy (the terminology varying with the specific circumstances), entail a relative decoupling of capitalist practices from their national institutional embedding and, thus, an escape from the reach of democratically voiced demands. This escape means, in contrast to the first such experience, that the crisis could be addressed without – except for some cases – even temporarily abolishing democracy, but rather by transforming both democracy and capitalism.

Liberal society and citizen disaffection: capitalism and democracy after the 1970s

As we have seen before, this novel situation is sometimes seen as beyond the reach of critique (chapter 3). However, even the current capitalism is not entirely structureless, not merely based on communication flows and ever-changing networks, as is sometimes maintained. Its former institutional framework has largely been dissolved, but it will not remain without institutional embedding to which needs for justification can be attached. Similarly, democracy may have lost or weakened its major institutional foundation, the nation-state based on popular sovereignty. The realization of the claim to collective self-determination has become much more difficult in a situation in which no evident collectivity exists that both claims such autonomy and is capable of exercising it. However, this claim has not for that reason disappeared; in contrast, it may be more strongly voiced than ever – this is what the idea of 'democratization waves' is awkwardly referring to. We therefore need to review the constellation of democracy and capitalism after the most recent crisis and transformation.

If economic globalization means the relative decoupling of economic practices from the nation-state as the historical container of collective self-determination, this does not entail that these practices are entirely insulated from critique and demands, for at least three reasons. First, capitalism remains highly dependent on, and thus responsive to, the high-skill sector of the labour force (that sector from which demands of the 'third spirit' of capitalism arose, demands for autonomy and creativity). Secondly, capitalism remains dependent on large numbers of low-skilled, low-salary workers, which are now found globally, but not without repercussions, such as global mobility and demands for global justice. Thirdly, such global capitalism is crisis-prone in the absence of regulatory frameworks – globally, for instance, in terms of uncontrolled financial flows, regionally and sectorally in terms of adjustments and relocations that generate contestation.

Recent changes in democracy, in turn, appear to have resolved the governability and/or legitimacy crisis that at first seemed unresolvable. First, social demands were deferred either inconclusively, by reference to the absence of any alternative to obeying the rules of the economy, or by shifts to other actors, such as the translocation to supranational or intergovernmental institutions that are less exposed to legitimacy claims. This displacement endangers any commitment to collective self-determination and is accompanied by

the decline of programmatic mass parties that were expressing this commitment within the nation-state form. In turn,
we see the emergence of a media-driven aggregate-preference
democracy that was already long theorized by US political
science.[3]

Secondly, current European democracies are more inclined
to accept liberal-individualistic demands, from 'family policy'
issues such as divorce, abortion and gay marriage to broader
possibilities for individual self-realization in terms of practices of freedom of expression and communication of all
kinds. While much recent change may already appear to us
as normal and self-evident, we only need to recall the climate
of cultural consensus of the 1950s and 1960s with shared
norms and values created and enhanced by national public
cultural education and communication, such as in state
broadcasting and public schooling – once seen as an indis-
pensable precondition for inclusive democracy. The situation, though, is noticeably different in Southern democracies,
such as South Africa or Brazil to which we will turn in the
next two chapters.

Thirdly, this transformation of the relative emphasis on
social versus individual demands is accompanied by declining rates of formal political participation and increasing

[3] This observation stands in tension to the tendency, often observed,
of recent political thought towards widening the understanding of
democracy by emphasizing deliberation and participation over
consent and representation. And indeed, this tendency emerged
with the contestation of existing representative democracies from
the late 1960s onwards and has not subsided since. Our diagnosis
seems nevertheless valid for Northern democracies, given that the
emphasis on participation and deliberation remained confined to
academic debates and, with few exceptions, small strands within
the citizenry. In turn, Southern democracies present a different
picture. In numerous countries, disaffection with democracy has
not taken place, and the recent advent of inclusive democracy, as
in South Africa, or the return to it in Latin American countries,
has been accompanied by high-intensity participation and deliberation (to be addressed on pp. 114–15 and 138–44).

dissatisfaction with government performance in Europe (Offe 2009). The latter, though, has been until now rather inconsequential, leading to frequent election losses of government parties and the short-term rise of populist movements but not (yet) any major challenge to the acceptance of democratic rules.

In short, the way in which a democratic citizenry is connected to capitalist practices can no longer be fully captured by the formula 'welfare state and mass loyalty', which applied to the 1950s and 1960s, but rather by a new formula such as 'liberal society and citizen disaffection'. The situation described by that formula, though, is unlikely to be stable as it is highly problematic, for two distinct reasons.

On normative grounds, the abandonment of the principle of collective self-determination would transform modernity beyond recognition. Modernity is based on the commitment to both personal and collective autonomy and it requires some balance between the two. A situation in which the latter commitment becomes extremely weak does not appear to be sustainable over the medium and the long run. As a first example of what may turn out to be many to come, the attempt at resolving the current financial crisis among the European states that adopted the euro by imposing austerity policies on the, mostly Southern European, countries in budgetary difficulty has led to a socio-economically motivated mobilization not seen since at least the 1960s in Spain, Greece and some other countries. Speaking in functional terms, a savage global capitalism will enter into crises that create enormous social and ecological damage, some of which is already obvious today. The unsustainability of the lack, or weakness, of comprehensive regulatory mechanisms has persistently been argued by critics, from at least Karl Polanyi onwards, but is now highly visible. Movements for the 'self-defence of society' (Polanyi) have begun, reaching globally from the World Social Forum to Nobel award winners in economics, and the fact that their institutional impact has been minimal until now does not invalidate their significance, given the overall constellation.

In the near and medium-term future, remedies for the crisis-proneness of the current constellation of capitalism and democracy can be found in two directions. One possibility is technocratic re-regulation performed by political (and business) elites in intergovernmental ways (as sketched and argued by Majone 1996 and Scharpf 1999). Such solutions are certainly necessary, but they are also very likely to be insufficient and they can and will meet local and regional criticism and resistance because they will be designed in normatively problematic ways, not satisfying democratic criteria.

The other possibility, preferable but highly difficult to achieve, is the reconstitution of avenues of collective self-determination. In general, this is conceivable as either the revival of the nation-state as the political form that created the historical possibility of inclusive collective self-determination or the recasting of this possibility in different spatial terms, either larger, at regional or even global level, or smaller, as the self-defence of communities widely visible in Latin America. Each of these avenues has specific problems that make it less likely or less desirable or both. Global democracy, first, now mostly discussed under the term cosmopolitanism, seems most appropriate to a situation in which many economic practices have global extension or at least global consequences. However, there is extremely little historical experience of global deliberative practices so that the 'self', that is collectively supposed to determine its rules, barely exists.

The revival of the national political form, secondly, is in question because of the double fact that precisely this form was found insufficient with regard to global markets and furthermore saw its democratic qualities weakened in the face of the recent transformation of capitalism, as argued above. It may be viable under two conditions, though: these nation-states need to be large polities, with high levels of both production and consumption, that may therefore have sufficient economic leverage to withstand impacts from the global economy. And they need to be polities of forceful and recent democratization experiences so that the above experience of citizen disaffection after losses of legitimacy does not, or only in lesser terms, apply to them. In a combination of both reasons, as will be partly discussed below (in chapters 6 and 7), Brazil and South Africa may be such cases – much more than the United States or, until now, China, which fulfil the first but not the second criterion.

Finally, a regional reconstitution of democratic self-determination is what at least partially defines the project of European integration. The rather egalitarian federation of democratic polities to face common challenges in the present and for the future is a rare occurrence. Historically, we can point to alliances of city-states in ancient Greece or in the European Middle Ages, and more recently to the creation of the United States of America. In the present, however, European integration is the only case that has demonstrated significant advances in political integration and has for this reason sometimes been seen as a model for other world regions, for which, though, similarly favourable conditions do not seem to exist. More significantly, the inability of Europeans to act convincingly in the face of the politico-military and financial-economic crises of the first decade of the millennium has cast doubt even on European prospects. As a consequence, the citizen disaffection towards national politics in Europe could in general not be counteracted by a transfer of legitimacy to European Union institutions, with the temporary exception of some member countries, such as Portugal and Greece before the current crisis or to some extent Italy, and some policy areas, such as environmental policy or gender equality.

For present purposes, this sketch of possible futures in the connection between capitalism and democracy will have to suffice. The actual future will be a combination of all these elements, with a considerable likelihood of rather different avenues being pursued in different parts of the world and with a general risk of a continued weakening of the democratic character of our societies.

A constitutive tension between economic and political modernity

We have started our exploration of the relation between democracy and capitalism 'symmetrically', introducing the argument that these arrangements are both naturally compatible and that they are in contradiction with each other. The experiences of the past half-century seem to lean towards supporting the compatibility thesis, but we had to introduce significant concern about the quality of the kind of democracy that is compatible with capitalism. This latter step, thus, suggests that high-intensity democracy – inclusive and with high levels of deliberation and participation – does stand in a principled tension with capitalism, and maybe even with the predicament of economic modernity in general. In conclusion, we want to explore the reasons for such a concern.

Despite the loss of its model character for creating a new viable connection between capitalism and democracy, Europe remains attractive for people in many other parts of the world because of the comparatively forceful combination of work opportunities and protection from violence, persecution and poverty that it offers. Legal immigration into Europe, though, has been made extremely difficult – not to say impossible – for most people in the world, while illegal immigration under often life-threatening circumstances continues in the hope of a safer future life within Europe's boundaries. Legal and illegal immigrants are currently major contributors to the European economy, mostly in low-pay and low-qualification jobs in (often personal) services, mass production or home industry and (often seasonal) agriculture. Many of these economic Europeans do not have European citizenship and little prospect of acquiring it for themselves (with somewhat better prospects for their children). Thus, current European modernity operates with a tightly defined and rather closed concept of political membership in democracy whereas it simultaneously entertains a flexibly open understanding of economic boundaries, schematically as follows: protecting agricultural production, demanding free trade for industrial production, and selectively admitting labour without granting political citizenship.

Such asymmetric handling of economic and political membership constitutes a tension in the modern self-understanding. It may not be entirely without possibility of justification, but it is difficult to justify (for a discussion, see the chapter on 'membership' in Walzer 1983). If we consider political modernity as at least tending towards collective self-determination based on equal participation of all its members/citizens (inclusive democracy), then a plausible secondary assumption should be that such a modern polity satisfies its material needs, that is, it addresses economic matters, by also drawing on its citizens. Such an attitude is indeed expressed when one says that modernity differs most strongly from non-modern settings by rejecting slavery, i.e., in my terms, handling economic matters through non-citizens (Aldo Schiavone 1996 makes such an argument most forcefully).

If one looks at the history of the past two centuries – the centuries of the revival of the democratic commitment in the aftermath of the French Revolution – however, such doubly inclusive – political and economic – modernity was rather rare, and maybe best represented by the Scandinavian countries between the 1950s (or even the 1930s) and the 1980s. In most other circumstances, a significant part of the work for the satisfaction of material needs was performed by non-citizens: for much of the nineteenth century by non-enfranchised workers in Europe and slaves in the US or Brazil; for the twentieth century, by apartheid exclusion in South Africa; by colonial extraction in general; by imposing terms of trade by military or other means, such as in the combination of British and then US imperial domination and free-trade ideology; and most recently (again) through large-scale immigration of people who are not and will not easily become citizens.

Such a historical record seems to show that there is something we might call a constitutive problem of modernity, i.e., the inability of the most elaborate versions of political modernity to develop an inclusive/egalitarian – we may also say 'just' – way of dealing with economic matters. The democratic crisis of European capitalism, discussed above, marks paradoxically both the assertion of demands for collective self-determination, also with regard to economic matters, and the exit from a form of modern polity, the inclusive democratic welfare state, which developed relatively high levels of both economic and political inclusion. If we look beyond Europe, Brazil and South Africa have radically moved to inclusive and highly participative forms of democracy, but they struggle with elaborating an economic arrangement that is consistent with the political form, not least that enhances economic inclusion and reduces social inequality.

6

European and Non-European Trajectories of Modernity Compared

Varieties of postcolonial situations

The western sociological view of the 'modernizability' of societies has changed considerably over time. Around 1800, only Europe was modern and philosophies of history were employed to explain why this was and had to be so. By 1900, 'occidental rationalism' was no longer European but western, as Europeans could no longer deny the modernity of the USA, its having risen to outcompete much of Europe economically and to become a model of a democracy that the political classes of Europe were reluctant to embrace but had increasingly come to see as unavoidable. The early post-Second World War decades witnessed the systematic elaboration of the view that all the world could modernize, retaining though the idea that there was a considerable lag that separated the modernity of the USA from the 'modernizing' situations that prevailed almost everywhere else. Even though some authors reflected on the advantages of 'backwardness' (Gerschenkron 1962) that might allow latecomers to overtake early modernities, such surpassing was not foreseen in any near future. Thus, the ability of the Japanese economy to compete successfully with the North American one came as a surprise and a shock, leading gradually, as mentioned above, to reconsiderations of Weber's idea that a Protestant cultural background was essential for the rise of modern capitalism. By now, the successive developments in South Korea, Taiwan and most recently the People's Republic of China have consolidated into an 'East Asian model' for which some authors see the interventionist, developmental role of the state rather than cultural features as decisive. In contrast, it is still widely maintained that other regions of the 'Old World' keep failing to 'modernize', such as Arab and sub-Saharan African societies, and the reasons evoked often remain focused on cultural and religious factors (see Thomas 2011 for an overview of African historiography in the light of 'modernity').

This chapter will briefly outline an approach to the comparative study of modernities in terms of their 'societal self-understandings', rather than any unchangeable culture, and will exemplify it with brief discussions of Brazil and South Africa. The subsequent chapter (7) will deepen the analysis of South African modernity in its connection and contrast with European modernity.

The recent research on plural forms of modern socio-political organization has had a particular empirical focus on settings that lend themselves more to cultural–civilizational analysis than others do, to be explained against the basic assumptions held and methodologies preferred. Thus, considerable work has been done on the 'classic' civilizational areas, such as China, Japan and India. There is also relevant work on predominantly Islamic societies, but this work is strongly predetermined by the questions of whether modernity and Islam are compatible, in a culturalist vein or critical thereof, or what the obstacles to development in those societies are, in a neo-modernist vein. In all of these cases, the – prima facie plausible – assumption of radical cultural diversity between these regions and the alleged 'original' modernity of the West works so strongly in favour of culturalist or neo-modernist approaches – the choice often depending more on the scholar than on the findings – that breakthroughs towards novel understandings of current global modernity are practically impossible at the current state of debate, despite all the merits of many of the existing studies. An important exception here is scholarship in cultural studies, in which, however, *problématiques* of modern self-understandings often tend to be dissolved into processes of 'glocalization' or 'hybridization', losing sight of the valid questions that stood behind 'Eurocentric' conceptual frames that underpinned colonial domination (as critically analysed by Chakrabarty 2000).

As suggested above (chapter 3), one way of advancing the comparative analysis of modernity is to focus on transformations of modernity over time, thus avoiding the issue of lack of connection between the modernities to be compared. In this chapter, we move to comparisons across space, and now the means for avoiding the issue of comparability is to focus on societies that were historically strongly connected to Europe. Thus, the question of the specificity of modernity comes immediately to the forefront in all cases of the 'founding of new societies', to use the formula that Louis Hartz (1964) employed for the analysis of societies in which groups of colonial settlers interacted with native populations, in obviously highly asymmetric ways, in the institution of new societies. While the colonial period mostly goes back to the sixteenth and seventeenth centuries, the actual founding of societies often occurred at the turn of the eighteenth to the nineteenth century in conjunction with the Enlightenment and the French Revolution and sometimes in conscious application of social contract theories (for the notion of a 'world crisis' during the period 1780–1820, see Baily 2004 and below, chapter 8). Thus, there is no doubt about the modernity of such newly founded, indeed first post-colonial societies in terms of commitment to collective self-determination. At the same time, the terms of the contract, so to say, often deviated considerably from the European or French understandings, in the light of the particular situation in those societies, and the 'contracts' kept undergoing changes as a result of further experiences (e.g., Beilharz 2008; Lake 2008). In other words, post-colonial societies of this kind are, on the one hand, clearly analysable in terms of their ways of handling the modern *problématiques*, but, on the other, they have embarked on historical trajectories that vary considerably from the European one (for a detailed discussion of Hartz's approach, see Wagner forthcoming).

Among the 'new societies' of this kind, only the United States has long been the object of sustained scholarly debate about societal 'self-understandings', as proposed above (chapter 4), to a significant degree taking off from Louis Hartz's earlier – and much better known – work, the identification of individualist liberalism as the societal self-understanding of the United States (Hartz 1955). This analysis has been widely debated and, at some distance, been opposed by, first, an insistence on the republican tradition in the American self-understanding (Pocock 1975) and, second, by the identification of a plural communitarianism on a liberal background (Walzer 2001) as the twentieth-century self-understanding of the United States. Significantly, these responses to Hartz, as important as their contribution to political theory has been, have largely ignored both the native population of North America and the African-Americans as forced settlers, and they have thus provided a very partial view of the American self-understanding. In this sense, they fall behind the much earlier study of 'the American dilemma' in which Gunnar Myrdal (1944) aimed at analysing what was then known as 'the Negro question' in terms of an 'American creed' (as a remedy, see now Henningsen 2009).

The strong interest in the North American self-understanding is related to the long-dominant position of the US in world politics and the hegemonic position of its own, rather particular, modernity; and its particular expression needs to be understood against the background of the almost accomplished extinction of native Americans and the dominated position of African-Americans, who as the most sizeable minority in the US are predominantly of lower class and thus have had considerable difficulties in making their voices heard. Weak scholarly interest in other 'new societies', with the exception of area specialists, needs to be explained in a different way. These societies were too dominated by the European settler groups to find a strong interest in post-colonial studies, which have focused on South Asia and, to some extent, on decolonized African societies. In turn, these have been analysed by modernization theorists mostly because of their 'delay' in modernization that was in need of explanation – this holds in particular for Latin American societies that looked sufficiently 'western' to raise develop-mentalist expections but then fell short of fulfilling them. Or alternatively, Marx-inspired analyses, often from within these societies, developed critiques of modernization theory but without elaborating new angles on modernity. In the perspective developed here, in contrast, it is precisely because of this ambiguous position that the study of 'new societies' can not only generate novel insights about their trajectories but also trigger conceptual innovation in social and political theory and in comparative–historical and political sociology.

Among the 'new societies', South Africa and Brazil are particularly suitable choices for an innovative analysis of the plural trajectories of modernity as they share some features that support an analysis in the proposed terms. First, both societies show particularly pronounced and complex rela-tions between the various population groups, a fact that has enhanced the need of these groups to consciously reflect on their own societal self-understanding. Secondly, both soci-eties have initially adopted rather specific political forms, addressing the particularity of their colonial experiences in terms of both the external relation to the 'mother country' (or countries, in the case of South Africa) and the internal relations between the population groups. Thirdly, both societies have responded to further experiences through post-colonial transformative reinterpretations of their initial self-understanding and by developing a conscious self-understanding or even 'project' of their own particular modernity. Fourthly, in both societies, the most recent phase of fully inclusive democracy showed features of a particu-larly pronounced societal reflexivity (epitomized by the

Brazilian transformations leading up to the Porto Alegre World Social Forum in one case, and by the Truth and Reconciliation Commission in the other), having had strong repercussions in global debate. But, fifthly, both societies also show extremely high social inequality and accept the urgency of addressing this situation, not least in the face of widespread violence and crime. And finally, both societies have experienced considerable industrial development and have, at times, consciously deployed economic policy strategies, making them important actors in the current global context.

At the same time, there are numerous fundamental differences between South Africa and Brazil, and, as in the case of similarities, these are differences that lend themselves to comparatively elucidating the conditions for the formation of societal self-understanding. We can identify some general aspects and then further differentiate, according to the ways in which the basic *problématiques* are addressed. The general aspects concern the early tie to the mother country and the nature of the 'colonial encounter' (Asad 1995) between the population groups.

Brazil emerged from a conscious, state-driven colonization project and long remained subordinated to Portugal, whereas the first Europeans settled in South Africa to support long-distance trade without a colonization project. These settlers, in particular the first group, of Dutch origin, who became the Afrikaners, soon developed a collective identity, disconnected from their origins (Thompson 1964, 2006). Brazilian colonization originated, as in most other cases, in the settlement of one group of Europeans on territory inhabited by a native population. The situation changed drastically when, for economic reasons, large numbers of Africans were forced to resettle in Brazil and work as slaves, creating a society composed of members of three distinct origins. While the latter also holds for South Africa in general terms, this society witnessed originally a highly conflictual relation between two European settler groups, the Dutch and the British. The former, in particular, fought the native population in frontier zones, but both groups otherwise relied on dominated

Africans for domestic or farm work and services. In South Africa, too, economic development, in this case gold and diamond mining, altered the relationship between groups, as the industrial work of large numbers of Africans transformed domestic subservience into class relations.

In this context, we can discern some key elements of the – highly different – ways in which the basic *problématiques* of modernity were addressed.

The epistemic *problématique*

As a statist project, Brazil 'inherited' Christianity from Portugal as its official religion, and, in particular, a version of neo-Thomism as a social and political philosophy that started out as a kind of social contract but emphasized order and hierarchy, while at the same time allowing for pragmatic arrangements in everyday situations (Morse 1964: 153–8). As a planned intervention, Christian colonization embarked on a debate about the nature of the native populations and integrated them, in principle, into the Christian understanding of humanity. Thus, (religious) knowledge resources were employed to guide social and political action on the basis of a concept of humanity that embraced hierarchy without strong boundaries. From the late nineteenth century onwards, the expectation of superior knowledge guiding societal developments was translocated to the sciences, particularly to the comprehensive approaches of the social sciences (Schwartzman 1991).

In contrast, there was no common project, and no pronounced higher knowledge base either, in South African colonization, which was economically founded – initially in commercial terms, then in terms of agricultural subsistence for the first colonists. The relations to the African population were dominated by military control and economic exploitation, without much further concern about 'the other' (even though there was some Christian-Calvinist justification of principled inequality). With the growing interdependence of the groups resulting from industrialization, and in particular with the downward social mobility of the Afrikaner group after the South African War, the weakness of the epistemic basis of social life became problematic. A 'scientific' theory supporting the 'racial' segregation that already existed, and even demanding the formal separation that became known as apartheid, was developed with a marked contribution from sociology, in particular Afrikaner authors (Jubber 2007; Coetzee 1991).

The political *problématique*

In terms of independent states, Brazil emerged in the form of a constitutional monarchy in 1822 and was transformed into a republic in 1889, while the Union of South Africa in 1910 was the result of the unification of several polities of highly different composition and rule within the British Empire. While the former, in terms of citizenship regime, can at first sight be regarded as following the gradual path towards evermore inclusive democratization not unlike European societies, the latter witnessed increasingly entrenched segregation along with massive denial of rights, including political rights, in particular for the African population. Prior to the return to democracy after a military regime in Brazil and to the end of apartheid in South Africa, the political class in both societies had developed particular mechanisms of 'inclusion' and 'representation': in Brazil, mass union-centred corporatism, and in South Africa, the rule through leaders of the segregated groups and 'states'. Such mechanisms came to a radical end with the introduction of equal universal suffrage in South Africa, a major political rupture in this society, and have become increasingly inoperative in Brazil, due to the weakening of the unions in the recent neo-liberal phase of capitalism and the emergence of 'insurgent citizenship' (Holston 2008) in Brazilian urban centres. In both cases, recent changes have created novel kinds of political problems, for which new solutions are being sought, often by adapting the former model, but clearly have not yet been found (Domingues 2008; Larrain 2000).

Significantly, as alluded to above (chapter 5), we may witness in these societies the transformation of 'low-intensity democracy', which was also long considered functionally adequate for Europe and the US, into more participatory forms of democracy.

The economic *problématique*

The economic situation in both Brazil and South Africa is marked by the availability of resources and thus actual and potential wealth, but also by export dependency and by weak redistribution policies, leading to high social inequality. In both cases, as mentioned above, the societal significance of the 'racial' question increased for economic reasons because of slave import in Brazil and internal migration of Africans to production sites in South Africa. Only in South Africa, though, did a horizontally stratified system of largely endogamous classes emerge due to segregation, whereas 'inter-ethnic' relations have been much more widespread in Brazil with a looser correspondence of skin colour to social class – as well as an official disinterest in this question. Both societies aimed to move towards greater self-sufficiency, in Brazil in the form of import substitution policies inspired by dependency theories, in South Africa in response to the – always incomplete – isolation imposed by sanctions against the apartheid regime, but both have also revised these policies more recently (Domingues 2008).

In both societies, the elites – composed and defined in highly different ways – have long practised a societal organization that depended economically on a majority of the population that was not enfranchised in terms of citizenship. Lack of formal juridico-political citizenship persisted in South Africa until the end of apartheid; in Brazil, formal criteria for dividing the population being historically less pronounced and today absent, the exclusion from political citizenship gradually ceased to exist, but exclusion from social citizenship remains strong. In both cases, the key challenge resides in radically transforming the old model of societal organization. From this brief, conceptually driven account, though, it should already have become clear that meeting this challenge is not 'merely' a matter of a new economic profile (Salais and Storper 1993) and stronger socio-economic redistribution. What seems to be required – and what is actively being sought in both societies – is a new arrangement of modernity that includes novel forms of (social and political) knowledge as well as novel understandings of citizenship, participation and representation – thus, new answers to the epistemic and political *problématiques*, too (see Santos 2006/7).

Comparing non-European and European varieties of modernity

After this brief sketch, it is possible to indicate the contours of the comparison between non-European and European trajectories of modernity with a view to opening a perspective on plural forms of modernity that emphasize interpretation of patterns of meaning without relying on a concept of civilization that seems to be too loaded with historical and theoretical burdens to be fruitful today.

It is part of the 'classic' European self-understanding that polities are in control of their territory and are built by, and on the foundation of, homogeneous populations. These are basic assumptions behind the concepts of, first, state sovereignty and, then, popular sovereignty (even though federalism should not be underestimated as an alternative option long fallen into oblivion). The idea of homogeneity could be expressed alternatively or complementarily in civic, cultural, linguistic, or ethnic terms, but in each case this assumption both alleviated and guided the search for answers to the *political problématique*. The subsequent problems of citizenship and representation were addressed through mostly slow and gradual extension up to equal universal suffrage in the former case (often reached only by 1919, in some cases after the Second World War), and through social cleavage-based formation of political parties in the latter.

The *economic problématique* was 'modernized' in Europe by the idea that extension of the commercial bonds between human beings would either pacify societies or maximize their wealth or both. This thinking inspired the market revolution from the late eighteenth century onwards. Experience with market self-regulation, however, solicited reinterpretations of this idea, which were put forward in a great variety of ways from the second half of the nineteenth century onwards, all entailing some kind of non-market organization of national economies. These novel responses not only rearticulated the economic and political *problématiques*, in terms of creating the 'states versus markets' debate, they also entailed the inclusion of the working classes (and sometimes the female population) into the polity, as the period of economic 're-regulation' coincided with the period of extension of citizenship (as discussed in chapter 5).

Both the original and the revised interpretations of the political and the economic *problématiques* drew on resources provided by the handling of the *epistemic problématique*. In the seventeenth century, European modernity referred to natural rights as a basic orientation. The dissolution of the old regimes, which could no longer be justified, however, created high contingency and radical uncertainty, in response to which new kinds of knowledge were produced, in particular theories about the social bond that sustained some notions of likely order even under conditions of self-determination. The theories of the commercial bond were mentioned above; theories of the cultural-linguistic bond sustained efforts to solve 'the national question' and create homogeneity; and theories of social interest-based bonds, solidaristic as in Durkheim or antagonistic as in Marx, pushed towards solving 'the social question'. Significantly, the inter-war years of the twentieth century saw 'collective existentialisms' (Agnes Heller) emerge from both the 'national' and the 'social' debates, underpinning the rise of totalitarianisms.

It was only in the post-Second World War period that the radical interpretations were defeated and withdrawn or moderated in Western Europe. The new polities worked with some compromise of liberal, national and social ideas and hoped to bind those ideas together with a more technocratic version of social science as an epistemic reference point. Many observers agree that this model entered a new crisis with new needs for reinterpretation. Debates about neoliberalism, globalization or individualization are indicators of the dissolution of the model, but they do not indicate directions for new responses, not least because they underestimate the role of collective agency and creativity (Karagiannis and Wagner 2007). At this point, the trajectories of South Africa and Brazil meet with that of Europe. In the former societies, radical transformations are ongoing, whereas in Europe the predominant – and far from insignificant – response is regional integration, often pursued in the hope that more radical reinterpretations can be avoided. The European reinterpretations proceed from a position of superior power in the global context, but not necessarily from a position of richer cultural-interpretative resources at hand to find new answers. Precisely because crucial questions, such as those of internal homogeneity or of accomplished social inclusion, were considered closed and stabilized in Europe, the European social imaginary may have difficulties in reopening those issues and finding new solutions. A truly global sociology of modernities will need to consider Europe a particular case among others, not least so as to be able to retrieve all the resources that might be needed for arriving at solutions that are at least temporarily superior to the old ones. In the final two chapters, we will try to advance towards such a world sociology, first by deepening the comparative approach by focusing on the similarities and differences between European and South African modernity (chapter 7), and, in a second step, by drawing some more general conclusions for a world sociology of modernity (chapter 8).

7

Violence and Justice in Global Modernity: Reflections on South Africa with World-Sociological Intent

Fifty years ago, around 1960, the widely accepted sociology of modernization divided the world into 'modern societies' and societies that still had to undergo processes of 'modernization and development'. After fundamental criticism of its evolutionist and functionalist assumptions, the theory was widely discredited two decades later. Its demise by 1980, though, has left the comparative sociology of contemporary societies with numerous problems. First, modernization theory has not been replaced by any other approach that aims at providing a sociological analysis of the global social configuration, despite all the talk about 'globalization'. Second, the critique of functionalist reasoning has deprived sociology of the means of assessing collective problem-solving capacity. As a consequence, neo-liberal economics and comparative-political economy have come to dominate this issue. Thirdly, the critique of evolutionism has tended to throw overboard all normative concerns in the sociological analysis of social configurations. As a consequence, normative political theory in various guises has tended to become more central than sociology in the assessment of contemporary socio-political constellations.

This chapter explores the 'conceptual relation' between the so-called modern societies of the 1960s and apartheid and post-apartheid South Africa over the past half-century with a view to elaborating elements of a new sociology of the global social configuration, or, in short, world sociology. Discussing at the outset the common assumption that a conceptual abyss separated apartheid society, which operated by means of violent oppression, from liberal–democratic societies, in which public action is in need of justification, the chapter insists instead on the need for a comparative–historical reconstruction of the trajectories of 'western societies', on the one hand, and South Africa, on the other, in their changing connectedness in the world context. It will be argued that violence has never been absent from the history of modernity and that concerns for justice can be expressed in more varied ways than much modernist thinking assumed. The comparative observations, furthermore, show that key questions of socio-political organization, such as the formation of a collective will, the relation between individual freedom and collective self-determination, and social justice, have not found permanent answers and that there is little reason to assume that the responses found in the 'old modernity' of the 1960s are superior to others in the current condition of global modernity.

From a 'western' point of view, the world of the early twenty-first century is dominated by a generalized discourse on human rights and democracy, which signals a liberal-individualistic conception of social life. Other voices are then portrayed either as expressing resistance for reasons of power or as failing to appreciate the world-historical achievements that the liberal paradigm produced. 'Social and political thought may have had the last conceptual revolution it needs,' as Richard Rorty (1989: 63) famously put it in his attempt at reconciling liberal, pragmatic and postmodern social and political theories. Rorty – whose dictum dates from the late 1980s – exempted from his view only a few socio-political situations, including prominently the case of apartheid South Africa where oppression and exploitation of one part of the population by the other persisted in an entirely unjustifiable way. Because of this exceptionality, according to Rorty, conceptual labour was likely to be fruitless in changing South Africa, and the recourse to violence was justified, even though elsewhere in the world it was not.[1]

Rorty's view can be, and has been, criticized on numerous grounds. For present purposes, his way of dividing the world into areas of different conceptuality is of particular interest. Significantly, his division is not a cultural one, such as Samuel Huntington's almost contemporaneous idea of a coming clash of civilizations, but one that contrasts normatively justified 'liberal institutions' with a non-liberal world in which violence reigns. Behind a postmodern facade, Rorty made strong claims about the absolute and inescapable reign of liberal modernity in our contemporary cosmology, regardless of historical and cultural difference. At the same time, Rorty's modernity is – even though in a slightly idiosyncratic way – nothing but the combination of commitments to individual self-realization and humanitarianism that was pioneered by the West. Despite some discussion of political community and solidarity, socio-political bonds are very thin in Rorty's universe. As we will try to show, this view is and remains rather specific to the recent experience of modernity

---

[1] For the relation between regimes of violence and those of justice, see Boltanski 1993. The concept of justice is used here in a broad sense, as referring to situations in which human action and institutional rules are subject to demands for justification (see in general Boltanski and Thévenot 1991). Such demands can be plural and they can change over time and across situations. In contrast, normative theories of justice in a more narrow sense try to elaborate a limited and coherent set of criteria for justice, in the tradition of John Rawls.

in some western countries, and it is not without contestation even there.

The following observations and reflections will take up the issue of apartheid South Africa's exceptionality but will not start from the assumption that this polity belonged to a different conceptual world. Rather, it will investigate differences and similarities to possibly identify South Africa's particular modernity – rather than its non-modernity during apartheid times.[2] To do so, a static perspective that will just recognize egalitarian-inclusive forms of political participation and social life in one case – the rule of modernity – and their absence and the imposition of power- and violence-driven forms of exclusion in the other – the exception – will not suffice. A historical-comparative approach is adopted that allows us to identify trajectories of socio-political change and to situate 'the exception' in the larger frame of world history, thus connecting historical observations and conceptual reflections to elements of a world sociology of modernity.

The lunar landing and the Sharpeville massacre

The early 1960s witnessed President Kennedy's announcement that the United States of America had embarked on a space exploration project that would allow them to land a man on the moon before the end of the decade. At the height of the Cold War, Kennedy was responding to the fact that the Soviet Union had been the first both to send a satellite into orbit – Sputnik in 1957 – and to enable a cosmonaut to circle the earth – Yuri Gagarin in 1961 – and his announcement was to lift the spirits in his own country,

---

[2] The following reflections emerge from ongoing research, and so may undergo modifications in more detailed future works. I would like to thank Jacob Dlamini for critical comments, which I hope are the beginning of an extended conversation.

by then used to being regarded as the leading nation of the world.

The early 1960s were also the peak period of decolonization in Africa, with 24 countries gaining independence between January 1960 and October 1962. It was the time when western sociologists, especially in the United States, spoke of their own societies as 'modern' and saw other societies in the world as being at different stages on the single evolutionary trajectory of 'modernization and development'. The South African government, though, bloodily repressed the call for liberty and equality in that country in the infamous Sharpeville massacre of 21 March 1960 in which police, mostly through gunshots, killed 69 people and injured over 180, including many women and children. The apartheid regime, which left the British Commonwealth one year later, thus demonstrated its determination to fight the trend of the time and to uphold its euphemistically named policy of 'separate development'.

The announcement of the lunar landing project conveyed the image of a society projecting itself into a future that meant endless progress, whereas the Sharpeville massacre signalled a world marked by oppression and violence from which there seemed to be no exit. This is an imagery that has long held sway in the western world, the 'First World' as it long saw itself, and despite considerable rethinking since the 1970s, it refuses to go away entirely. While it is reasonable to assume that there are indeed different collective ways of being-in-the-world, these differences can often more fruitfully be analysed as varieties of modernity rather than as marking the distinction between a modern world in which normative principles reign and in which practices need to be justified by recourse to those principles, on the one hand, and, on the other hand, a non-modern one in which power is exercised by means of violence and oppression.

The Sharpeville shooting triggered a global debate and led to the condemnation of the actions of the South African apartheid regime. However, the segregation of population groups had been common in the South African region since the late nineteenth century, and formal apartheid policy had been announced and introduced in the Union of South Africa after 1948. Between 1948 and the early 1960s, though, western governments were not particularly concerned about the matter, which was instead considered a domestic affair. Before the 1950s, in the colonial world, South Africa was a respectable member of the British Commonwealth and an ally in two world wars. In the view of the world public, thus, on a closer look, the exceptionality of the apartheid regime seems more the product of 'excessive' violence and oppression, whereas the 'normality' of exclusion and domination had been considered as, if not acceptable, at least not significant enough to warrant major debate or action. Today, in turn, South Africa is seen as a 'normal' democratic society based on a rather successful market economy and about to become a 'global player' in the world order of the twenty-first century. The distinction between the past exceptionality of apartheid and current normality, however, is insufficient to locate South African society and politics in the global context. The guiding idea of the following reflections is that an exploration of the historical trajectory of what we will call South African modernity will help understand both the specificities of South African society, its singularity, and the social transformations of the world over the past half-century – 'The year 1960 was a watershed in modern South African history' (Thompson 2006) – on which our analysis will focus after a brief consideration of earlier developments.

South Africa and the 'birth of the modern world'

The nineteenth century witnessed the birth of the view that Europe – or the West – was ahead of other regions on the evolutionary trajectory of world history, a view that would remain dominant way into the twentieth century until a few decades after the Second World War. Recent attempts at writing 'world history', however, have considerably qualified this view by showing that the rise of Europe to world domination during the nineteenth century was related to rather contingent events, not to a long history of progress in this region. The 'great divergence' (Pomeranz 2000) that separated Europe from the rest of the world by 1900 and was the most important background to the 'birth of the modern world' (Baily 2004), to quote only two of the most important recent such analyses, was most significantly related to two quite different occurrences: on the one hand, requirements of warfare in Europe led to superiority in military technology that, in turn, permitted asymmetric commercial relations, underpinned by the superior firing power of the Europeans. On the other hand, since the religious wars Europe had developed a whole new array of ideas about peaceful and mutually beneficial living together that gave rise to radical positions in social and political thought, such as individual rights, property rights, state and later popular sovereignty and market self-regulation. The experiences of the application of these concepts are so varied that they cannot and should not be adopted without qualification and amendments (an issue to which I will return below). However, they enlarged the space of political debate by introducing novel options from then on that needed to be addressed even by those who were opposed to them, even by those outside Europe. In other words, it is to some extent true to say that intellectual resources for invoking justice and the need for justification were elaborated and refined in European debates of the seventeenth and eighteenth centuries, and that the presence of such resources in Europe has had an impact on global developments. At the same time, though, the connections between Europe and other parts of the world were marked by violence and oppression – or more strongly, the Europe in which modern modes of justification arose engendered a different world situation elsewhere by means of violence and, as we shall suggest in conclusion, continues to rely on the latter as a condition for its own sustainability.[3]

The combined effect of these occurrences was to create the modern world as a world of colonial domination in which several types of (post-)colonial situation coexisted. Some colonies had already turned into independent states by the end of the eighteenth or beginning of the nineteenth centuries, thus at the height of the elaboration of the novel social and political concepts mentioned above. These societies (most in North and South America, later Australia and New Zealand) mostly had a majority or dominant population of European descent and have been referred to as 'new societies' because of the rather conscious act of collective self-foundation (Hartz 1964; see above, chapter 6). Those regions that are often referred to as classic civilizations (much of East and South-East Asia) were never fully colonized but

---

[3] The argument about the creation of situations of dependence and of periphery by the centres of political action is well known from, among others, dependency and world-systems theories. However, the version proposed here emphasizes the interplay between instrumental action and normative argument that was at work in creating both colonialism and the post-colonial world. I will not here be able, but hope to do so in later analyses, to fully address the question of 'non-western' sources of social and political knowledge that can and should be mobilized in the anti-colonial struggles, an argument often present in such struggles, in South Africa through the Pan-Africanist Congress, which had organized the Sharpeville demonstrations, and the black consciousness movement. The issue here is less the search for alternative bodies of knowledge as such, as regional 'philosophies', than the combination of forms of knowledge that arise from specific experiences and the openness towards conceptions of person, collectivity and being-in-the-world that avoid the individualist instrumentalism that emerged in the West. For a recent discussion of 'Southern theory' in relation to the knowledge claims of the 'metropole', see Connell 2007 and Santos 2007; for a view of individualist instrumentalism as an extreme interpretation of modernity, as 'imperial modernism', see Wagner (2008: ch. 11).

were dominated by European powers in commercial relations. And finally, societies with a majority indigenous population formed the colonies in the more narrow sense of the term, that is, societies that were politically controlled and mostly also administered by European powers until after the Second World War (most of Africa, South Asia, with some particularity in the Middle East and Northern Africa in the context of the disintegration of the Ottoman Empire).

South Africa is a rather special case that does not fit neatly into any of these categories[4]; rather, it comprises aspects of all of them. It witnessed the complex relation of two European settler groups, of Dutch and of British descent, in very different economic positions, agriculture for the former and commerce the latter, until the beginning of the twentieth century and the South African War. Indigenous polities long persisted in the territory that was later to be the Union of South Africa, only to be militarily defeated well into the nineteenth century. Small new polities were created by the 'Dutch', Afrikaans-speaking agricultural settlers, based on ideas of collective self-determination, but at the same time also on violent oppression and eviction of the indigenous population. This socially, culturally and economically multifarious setting was then radically transformed by, first, increasing seizure of land and, second, gold and diamond mining developments of global commercial significance. Despite the military victory of the British over the Afrikaners and some persistent disputes between the 'white' groups, this novel constellation led to a certain convergence of agricultural and commercial interests and, thus, to an alliance of the two European groups in organizing the domination of the other population groups that would become formalized

---

[4] Though Louis Hartz considered it a 'new society' and asked Leonard Thompson (1964) for a contribution on South Africa to his comparative endeavour. A typology of colonial situations was already proposed by Ribeiro (1971 [1969]: 79–89) as a starting point for a world sociology.

as apartheid from the middle of the twentieth century onwards.

Thus, South Africa combined the idea of collective, political self-determination – the aspect that justifies its analysis as 'new society' – with the idea of commercial and market society, highly integrated into the world market – the aspect that allows its sociological analysis in terms of the division of social labour and of class struggle. But it developed both of them with highly specific features of colonial oppression and exclusion, such as the formation of partially self-determined polities, first on parts of the territory, then by parts of the population, and the introduction of internal market barriers through restrictions on mobility and specific wage regimes, thus, we might say, with only partial market freedoms, despite the abolition of slavery. This was the version of modernity with which South Africa entered the second half of the twentieth century – a very particular one in its combination of features.

But was this a modernity at all – or was it rather a regime that defies the modern commitment to autonomy and mastery, to freedom and rationality? An equally brief review of the trajectory of European modernity from the 1800s to the end of the Second World War is required to balance the picture.

While there is little doubt that European intellectual innovations in the course of the seventeenth and eighteenth centuries emphasized the commitments to autonomy and mastery, and even that some institutional innovations between the 1780s and the 1830s aimed at safeguarding those commitments, the period from the middle of the nineteenth to the middle of the twentieth century demonstrated that any such casting into historical forms was much more problematic than initially envisaged (see chapter 1 above). There were basic tensions, such as the one between individual autonomy and collective autonomy, or the one between freedom and control. By the twentieth century, these tensions had become strongly visible in social life and political projects had emerged that insisted on the need to resolve them by exclusion and/or oppression. The 'national question' of the middle of the nineteenth century had been transformed into aggressive nationalism by 1900 and in some places into totalitarian projects based on ideas of the supremacy of one's own nation or people. The 'social question' of the mid-nineteenth century, to which the concept 'solidarity' had appeared to provide some compelling response for a long time, turned into sometimes violent class struggle, even civil war, and into a totalitarian project that emphasized the progressive historical mission of one class, the working class. These totalitarianisms, Nazism and Stalinism at the forefront, can be seen as radical interpretations of the modern commitment to collective self-determination through the planned transformation of society in the light of strong substantive ideas about history. Segregation and elimination of people were central parts of these radical projects. In more moderate versions, segregation, too, was often a key to solving problems of modern socio-political organization so that elimination could be avoided.

The autumn of European modernity and South African exceptionalism (1948–1961)

After the military defeat of Nazism and Stalin's death, these radical projects for transforming society were by and large abandoned in Europe, and concomitantly all substantively strong interpretations of modernity lost persuasiveness. Their successor modernity in Western Europe was characterized by two main features: on the one hand, the modern idea of planned transformation was emptied of – 'national' or 'social' – substance, but radicalized in terms of seeing the world as an object passively available to human intervention. Some strands of post-Second World War European philosophy were struggling to grasp these developments, often inspired by Edmund Husserl's earlier reflections on the 'crisis of the European sciences'. In the works of authors such as Martin Heidegger, Hannah Arendt and Jan Patočka, the decline of Europe and the concomitant rise of the US and of the Soviet Union meant a transformation of modernity in which the world had increasingly become the object of instrumental intervention rather than the dwelling-place of human beings. The movement of human beings into orbit was seen as exemplary for this transformation as it allowed the earth to be gazed at from the outside, to be placed in front of human eyes, and thus to be acted upon from the outside rather than from within. Mostly, this transformation was seen as both deplorable and irreversible, and those like Hannah Arendt who tried to retrieve intellectual resources from ancient debates were seen as pursuing an anachronistic endeavour. At the onset of decolonization, on the other hand, Europe was no longer the agent of any such imperial project of planned transformation – this role had precisely been taken by the USA and the Soviet Union – but concentrated on domestic perfection, 'internal colonization' as it was sometimes called, in building the inclusive democratic welfare states that claimed to combine full political participation with the provision of material well-being and social security.

Again, South Africa, now adopting apartheid as its main tool for socio-political organization, occupies a very particular position in this mid-century transformation of modernity. It clearly drew on the same debates about the national and the social question that had marked Europe. Its peculiarity in the 'national' sense resided in the fact that groups to be segregated were defined by skin colour rather than by language or culture, even though these latter features were seen to go along with skin colour. In the 'social' sense, economic developments had added a new layer of class division. Before the large-scale development of mining at the end of the nineteenth century, native Africans had worked as domestic or agricultural labourers in subservient positions wherever they had not succeeded in retaining earlier socio-economic structures in their own polities. Mining, however, created a large demand for labour power, and the white settlers secured the supply through the destruction of the viability of those structures and thus created a black working class that was not drawn towards capitalism by market logic but through legal-political coercion. Thus, South Africa retained forms of exclusion that were characteristic of nineteenth-century European modernity but were given their particular shape by the colonial politico-cultural and socio-economic setting. When European intellectuals of the early twentieth century diagnosed – and deplored – the rise of mass society as the upcoming inclusion of all residents of a territory in modern practices, white South Africans saw no reason to consider themselves as sharing the same fate. Rather, their particular condition seemed to allow for a substantive redefinition of modernity that preserved its restrictively applied normative features. Apartheid was a fully argued intellectual project for collective self-determination as 'separate development', and thus the cornerstone of South African modernity at the time.[5] Its very asymmetric terms were clearly veiling power relations and violating the modern commitment to equal liberty. They were not, though, fundamentally different from the reasons invoked by European nineteenth-century thinkers for denying political citizenship and socio-economic representation to women and workers. The fact that Europeans

[5] This is not to say that it was an intellectually coherent project nor that its implementation could simply be derived from a master plan – this has never been so for any historical variety of modernity. The historiography of South Africa has amply demonstrated the contingency of the rise of formal apartheid policies and the piecemeal nature of their implementation. (My thanks to Jacob Dlamini for insisting on this clarification.) What is to be underlined here, rather, is the existence of justifications for apartheid that to some extent convinced its supporters and also left an imprint on its opponents. Furthermore, those justifications for the singularly South African mode of restricted modernity, as we might say, created the space for critique in the name of a wider modernity based on equal liberty, such as that advocated by the African National Congress (ANC) from its foundation a century ago until its ban, the moment at which regime violence was to be counteracted by opposition violence. For a discussion of the relation between the rationale, justification and madness of apartheid, see Coetzee 1996.

were initially not particularly concerned about the oppressive nature of South African modernity can be explained in part by commercial interest. In addition, however, the motivations of the builders of apartheid were only too recognizable and understandable for European elites during the 1950s, given that they themselves had been forced rather than volunteered to abandon relatively similar approaches to socio-political organization not too long before.

'Problems of legitimacy' and 'governability crisis' in different settings (1961–1978)

The Sharpeville massacre showed everyone willing to see the degree of oppression and the lack of any sustainable justification for apartheid. As a consequence, both the resistance struggle within the country and at its borders, dominated by the exiled African National Congress (ANC), and international protests, often under the initiative of the United Nations, intensified. However strong the substantive foundations for apartheid may have been in earlier South African politics, they had proven to provide not even the minimum basis for a regime to be tolerable for large parts of the population. In reaction, the South African government increased the repression of opposition activities and at the same time strove to enhance its techniques of social management.[6]

---

[6] One other polity, founded in 1949 under otherwise very different circumstances, faced the similar problem of not having been able to secure sufficient legitimacy from its population by 1961 and thus took the radical step of fencing in the whole territory to prevent the 'exit' choice by significant numbers of its population (see Hirschman 1993 for an analysis in terms of exit, voice and loyalty). This polity was the German Democratic Republic, which built the Berlin Wall in August 1961 and ceased to exist in 1990, the same year in which Nelson Mandela was freed. In the global political context, ironically, the GDR supported the anti-apartheid struggle of the ANC, which had close links with the Soviet Union during the Cold War.

From the Rivonia trial of 1964 and the subsequent imprison-
ment of leading ANC members to the Soweto killings in
1976 and 1977, repressive measures became increasingly
violent and intolerant of every expression of dissent and
discontent, on the one hand. On the other hand, segregation
was meant to be perfected through the creation of 'independent homelands' and further resettlement activities for
the latter, of which District Six of Cape Town became an
example of symbolic significance. District Six had been a
residential and commercial area with a socio-economically,
ethnically and religiously very mixed population close to
the city centre of Cape Town. In 1966, it was declared a
'whites-only' area and from 1968 onwards its non-white
residents were removed and resettled in the area of the Cape
Flats, far away from the city. Based in, and justified by,
broader urbanistic concerns, this action was exemplary for
the technocratic implementation of apartheid policies during
this era in which the 'higher' justification of 'separate development' had already lost credibility.

Specific as the District Six resettlement was, it was not
without parallels in other parts of the world. The current
exhibition on the history of the area in the District Six
Museum in Cape Town, as at December 2010, includes in
one corner a display on urban renewal policies in the southern Swedish city of Malmö. This is done without further
explanation – because the parallels are striking. European
modernists had often, and increasingly during this period,
resorted to the clearing of dense urban districts based on
concerns for public health and social reform, and these measures had mostly, maybe always, also entailed the segregation
of lower, potentially 'dangerous', classes from the respectable
urban population.

The 1960s were the heyday of 'organized modernity'
throughout the western part of the world (Wagner 1994).
Justification shifted from substantive concerns of various
kinds to the efficient management of public affairs, importantly including a managed crisis-free economy that would
in turn provide the means for limited redistribution policies

aiming at broad social security and concomitantly 'mass loyalty' (Narr and Offe 1975). In the course of the decade, however, it became clear that efficiency and security could not fully replace other substantive concerns, even though political thinkers argued evermore forcefully that efficiency as such can provide legitimacy (for a contemporary critique, see Habermas 1968, and for recent elaborations of the approach Majone 1996, Scharpf 1999). Other concerns, in particular the one for self-realization, were to be fully acknowledged but should be seen as private and based in individuals or groups, rather than as public and collective, so that a liberal polity without strong claims to substantive collective self-determination would be entirely adequate (Rawls 1971). Increased discontent from the end of the 1960s onwards showed such views to be erroneous in practice in the West, whatever their conceptual merit may have been. The contestations were diagnosed as leading to 'legitimacy problems' (Habermas 1973) and a 'crisis of governability' (Crozier et al. 1975) in the so-called advanced industrial democracies, as discussed above (chapter 5). In South Africa, such views were not very persuasive in the first place, since the technocratic intensification of apartheid could not succeed in masking the denial of collective self-determination and full socio-economic inclusion and was accompanied by the intensification of oppression through police and military measures. The crisis of governability and legitimacy, to use those terms, was much stronger and needed to find a more radical response in a regime change.

The democratic crisis of apartheid and capitalism (1978–1989/94)

From the late 1970s onwards, both South African and western modernity underwent radical transformations. In Western Europe and the United States, briefly, the contestations of the late 1960s and their politically rather limited outcomes during the 1970s[7] ushered in a broad critique of attempts at planned social change, and even of the possibility of planned social change at all. The structure of such argument has been neatly synthesized by Albert Hirschman (1991) in terms of a 'rhetoric of reaction' that emphasizes either the futility of attempts at change or their perversity in terms of unintended consequences or the fact that any tinkering with socio-political arrangements might jeopardize the historical accomplishments of modernity.[8] This argument was accompanied by two other ones, of which one can be regarded as a conclusion to the former, and the other as one of its conditions. First, if planned social change is futile, perverse or dangerous, then social life should be left to mechanisms of self-regulation, without steering by any kind

[7] The emphasis in this assertion is on *political* change in a more narrow sense, change in the nature of democracy, as discussed above in chapter 5. Let it at least be noted that protest-induced changes were highly significant in three areas: women achieved full legal equality and greater rights to determine their lives through reforms of civil and penal law codes in general and more liberal regulation of divorce and abortion in particular. These changes, second, can be seen as part of moves to increase the space for individual self-realization, also already touched on above, otherwise recognizable in the end of state monopoly (or strong hegemony) in schooling, public broadcasting and other areas. Thirdly, communication between public administration and citizens changed from being authoritarian in style towards being oriented towards rights-holding citizens and, mostly somewhat later, paying customers.

[8] While Hirschman rightly labels these arguments conservative and reactionary, one needs to underline that authors who see themselves as critical (or progressive) can succumb to making use of them. This is, for instance, true for Pierre Bourdieu's argument about the structural limits of attempts to diminish educational inequality or for Claus Offe's critique of European integration in the name of normative accomplishments of the European nation-state (see also our discussion of Offe's notion of political progress, in chapter 3 above).

of authority. This argument has been fully developed in terms of the critique of Keynesian-style demand management and the return to the idea of market self-regulation, but it has broader social connotations as well. Second, a major reason why planning social change is seen as futile, perverse or dangerous resides in the very fact that an authority of some kind tries to implement its vision by proposing it to, or imposing it on, a population (or 'society') with which it is not identical. Thus, in contrast to traditional views of democracy as government by the people, such thinking applies the view that even democratic government is at best 'for' the people but not 'by' the people (see Karagiannis 2010 for a critical discussion). In more basic theoretical terms, this is a critique of the possibility of collective agency, of the possibility that a collectivity of human beings can act together, and that such action can be effected on itself. There is a long tradition of critique of 'collective concepts', and from the 1970s onwards it gains particular force in combination with the observable phenomena of, as they were known, the 'decline of the working-class' and the 'decline of the nation-state', thus capturing with 'class', 'nation' and 'state' three of the arguably most significant collective concepts of the nineteenth and twentieth centuries (see Wagner 2011 for more detail). As a result, sociological observers speak of strong trends towards individualization in contemporary western societies and sometimes even of a 'new individualism' (for different perspectives, see Buchmann 1989; Ferry and Renaut 1988; Honneth 2004b).

If analysed from a policy perspective, the attempts both at implementing and reinforcing apartheid up to the 1970s and at reforming and moderating it from the late 1970s onwards 'failed' in very much the same way in which expanded welfare state policies failed in Europe and the United States and were critically analysed as such (Wittrock 1983; Wagner et al. 1991 for an overview). However, South African society experienced legitimacy and governability problems in the presence of a forceful collective counter-project, embodied by the ANC in its alliance with the trade union organization COSATU and the South African Communist Party (SACP), which was powerful enough to undermine policy capacity but not in the institutional position to design state policies. Thus, any signs of crisis and failure did not necessarily lead to conclusions about collective agency in general, of state, nation or class, but in the first instance to conclusions about the inadequacy of the existing apartheid institutional arrangement to exercise planned social change in and on a society with which it was not identical.

In other words, while both western societies and South Africa may be said to have undergone a democratic crisis during the 1970s and 1980s, this crisis was interpreted in highly different terms. In the West, the limits of existing democracies were tested by movements of contestation, and calls for further 'democratization' were made to overcome these limits. However, the medium-term response was a transformation of political and economic arrangements such that performance expectations were lowered. The arguments about the decline of the nation-state and the crisis of the welfare state provided exactly this: reasons why governments and the economy should not be overburdened with (democratic) demands they cannot fulfil.[9] As a consequence, after a decade or so of rich and vivid debates, rather than further democratization a lower-intensity democracy emerged in which citizen disaffection was pronounced but usually remained rather inconsequential (see above, chapter 5). In

---

[9] Connell (2007: 153–5) suggests that rather similar developments took place in Latin America with the acceptance of the neo-liberal turn in economic policy. She seems to overlook or underestimate, however, the emergence of 'high-intensity' democracy in some countries, most pronouncedly Brazil, and the rethinking of citizen–polity relations in general, introducing notions of 'pluri-national' polity and indigenous rights that are highly transformative of a standard liberal understanding of the polity (for observations on the long tradition of 'attenuated liberalism' in Latin America, see Mota 2010).

South Africa, in turn, the fact that the ANC and its allies were offering a full programmatic alternative to the apartheid regime but were deprived of any possibility of implementing it raised high expectations for the moment at which this situation would change. Here, inclusive democracy was claimed in a non-democratic setting, and its advent was therefore seen as the very beginning of the exercise of collective self-determination in this society. Political change towards collective autonomy was the precondition for general social change.[10]

Democracy and society in South Africa after apartheid (1994–present)

With the adoption of free and equal universal suffrage, South Africa moved towards inclusive democracy, and the 1994 election victory of the ANC-based alliance confirmed the expectation that such constitutional change would lead to radical political change, due to the sudden enfranchisement of the majority of the population. South Africa is one of very few cases in which such radical political transformation occurred in a society with a world-market competitive economy, an efficient central state apparatus and other institutions that are usually referred to as key characteristics of

[10] Critical analysis in South Africa suggested for some time that South African capitalism required the particular form of exploitation that apartheid provided so that anti-apartheid struggle was necessarily anti-capitalist struggle, seeing in the Marxian tradition economic phenomena as the most fundamental aspect of the social world. 'Liberal' theorists, in turn, suggested that apartheid constituted a fetter to the fuller development of capitalism because of the renunciation of reaping the full potential of the 'human resources' of the country. In general, it seems more appropriate to say that capitalism can flourish under different socio-political conditions, and take different forms according to those conditions (see Lipton 2007 for a recent discussion of this debate).

'modern societies'.[11] This transformation – utterly unexpected even shortly before it occurred – is often considered a 'miracle', both because of the presumed unwillingness of a long-term successful elite to relinquish power and because of the presumed inability of a majority-based opposition without experience of administering 'functional' institutions to take power suddenly. The closest comparison in those terms is the transformation of authoritarian and oppressive Imperial Germany into the most participatory and most socially committed democracy of the time within a few weeks in the winter of 1918/19, leading initially to electoral majorities committed to socialism. The Weimar Republic, though, would witness the rise of Nazism in the wake of the world economic crisis of 1929 and it collapsed on Hitler's coming to power in 1933, after only fourteen years of existence.[12]

We may well accept that there is something miraculous about the South African transformation, maybe most significantly with regard to the personalities and abilities of key protagonists, in particular Nelson Mandela. However, specificities can nevertheless be noted that go some way towards understanding the recent years. First of all, it should be recalled, because later developments tend to consign this fact to oblivion, that the years of the transition were not peaceful at all. Violence, including state-supported violence, was quickly rising and spreading across society during the years when the future shape of society and politics was not yet clear and mistrust prevailed among the groups and parties about the sincerity of the declared intentions.[13] Second, the

[11] We may just recall that the first-ever transplant of a human heart was performed in Cape Town in 1967, thus giving evidence of the quality of medical expertise in apartheid South Africa.

[12] Thanks are due to David Cooper for extended discussions of this comparison.

[13] Among the numerous accounts of the end of apartheid, we single out Gevisser (2009), with an emphasis on the role Thabo Mbeki, later successor to Nelson Mandela as president of South Africa, played in enhancing communication between the opposed groups.

gradually emerging agreements were possible, despite decades of warfare and violent oppression, because a sense of the limits of apartheid and the need for reforming/overcoming it was widespread and communicatively shared relatively widely. Thus, to use currently common terminology, there was a civil society in which alternatives could be created and diffused. Thirdly, the actual transition itself was 'contracted' with a clear sense of key problems, maybe most importantly the need to both – and simultaneously – maintain the functioning of institutions and accept and preserve the legitimacy of the new political order. Finally, the ANC-based governing alliance is aware of the potentially difficult relation to its own electorate, as expectations about post-apartheid society are high and always at risk of disappointing – as has happened to some extent with regard to the efficacy of local administration and the persistence of high inequality. In these latter two respects, the simple but far from self-evident fact should be noted that this transformation is taking place with the awareness and knowledge of earlier, comparable transformations, thus that some of the crucial problems are known to a degree that they were not, say, in Weimar Germany.[14]

Observations about the past two decades can be used to point to some of the key issues in the further elaboration of South African society's persistently particular modernity. Primarily and centrally, South African modernity, as we have seen above, is strongly committed to collective self-determination in its attempt at redirecting socio-political organization away from apartheid exclusion and oppression. In the history of western modernity, the emphasis on collective self-understanding was based on some idea of the unity of the people – often specified as the nation – that concealed the underlying tension between the multitude of human beings of which any collectivity is composed and the

[14] That is why revolutions cannot be fruitfully compared without regard for their historical moments, as Theda Skocpol (1979) tried to do; see the debates between her (Skocpol 1994) and William Sewell (1994, 1999).

supposed emergence of a common will as required by the concept of popular sovereignty. In South Africa, this tension is plainly evident since democratic South Africa emerges from the domination of its majority population by a minority population group that, nonetheless, remains a part of the redefined collectivity. The tension is visible in former President Thabo Mbeki's characterization of South Africa as a society of two nations, one black and one white, or in the association of the use of Afrikaans with the history of oppression, thus singling out one of the two predominantly white language communities as the former oppressor.[15] In turn, the creation of the term 'rainbow nation' by Archbishop Desmond Tutu, a key figure in the transition, was meant to symbolize current unity in diversity, thus a situation in which different cultural orientations can coexist without threatening the basic commonality – of a 'nation' – that is required for forming and sustaining a democratic polity. The symbol of the rainbow was meant to go together with the practices of the Truth and Reconciliation Commission (TRC) which was charged with reviewing past violence and injustice and designing and implementing measures for compensation. Despite the achievements of the TRC, as impressively narrated by Antjie Krog (1998), the terms 'rainbow' and 'reconciliation' are both currently used rather as things that are yet to be accomplished and for which the considerable requirements have by no means yet been met.[16]

Second, the current democratic condition of collective self-determination was reached at least partly as a result of a struggle that was seen as national liberation on the model of similar struggles in other former colonies in Africa (for a discussion of the reasons for the end of apartheid, see Lipton 2007). The agent of struggle was the ANC-based alliance, which for this reason is seen – and sees itself – as the key

---

[15] For a demonstration of how lived experience may differ from political analysis of oppression, see Dlamini 2009.

[16] See Krog 2009 for an attempt at thinking the issue from a white and Afrikaans viewpoint in much more radical terms.

agent of future collective self-determination. The ANC has repeatedly gained an absolute majority in post-apartheid elections, even coming close to a two-thirds majority that would allow changes to the Constitution. The only major exception is the province of the Western Cape and some municipalities, including the city of Cape Town, which currently are governed by the Democratic Alliance (DA), a party that emerged from white opposition to apartheid and sees itself as a civic liberty-minded opposition to lasting uncontrolled one-party rule. Thus, South Africa faces a political situation that in one respect is similar to other African polities after the end of colonization: the agent of national liberation becomes the organized site for collective self-determination, thus marginalizing the role of elections and parliament in what comes close to being a one-party democracy (for a discussion, see Chabal 2009), in contrast to European democracies, and retaining a strong substantive pre-determination of the scope of collective action, in contrast to the standard liberal understanding. In contrast to other African polities, however, the dominant party is itself an alliance in which considerable difference of opinion and relatively pronounced public debate exist, and, furthermore, the successful presence of the DA in particular allows for persistent opposition politics and at least the regional elaboration of a government alternative (for a recent overview of South African party politics, see Butler 2010). Thus, we recognize here a particular positioning of the South African polity between a republicanism that allows a strong substantive direction of political action but can be criticized as a 'tyranny of the majority' (Tocqueville), on the one hand, and, on the other hand, a liberalism that emphasizes individual autonomy in terms of both civil rights and pursuit of opportunities, but can be criticized for neglecting the current impact of past oppression and exclusion and for aligning itself too easily with current global economic ideology.

This latter possibility leads, thirdly, to the particular relation between political equality and social solidarity that exists in South African debates and practices. As has been argued, the viability of democracy may depend on relations of trust within the citizenry that are also the source of solidarity, that is, the willingness to support others in need on the assumption of similar commitment to the polity and thus trust in the fact that one would find support oneself if in need (Offe 1998; for a broader discussion of changing forms of solidarity, see Karagiannis 2007). Rather than an option that can be more or less strongly pursued, the reduction of inequality through organized solidarity may thus be a precondition for sustaining South African democracy. Apartheid was a political regime of exclusion that sustained an economic regime of exploitation and impoverishment, identifiable through wage differences between black and white workers, infrastructural underprovision of townships and lack of concern for rural regions that were considered merely as flexible reservoirs of labour (see Seekings and Nattrass 2006 for a long-term analysis). As a consequence, apartheid South Africa combined political dominance by a minority with extremely high social inequality. Anti-apartheid struggle focused on political inclusion as the most visible and most easily identifiable feature of apartheid (and the one that let external condemnation by the West emerge – and by liberal philosophers who had little to say about social solidarity), but the expectation was that a change to an inclusive democratic political regime would also quickly improve the living conditions of the majority. This, though, has quite clearly not happened to the expected degree, and discontent with the persistence of poverty and inequality, including now marked inequality within the black population due to the creation of groups of successful black business people and politicians, is strong. The commitment to political equality remains uncontested, and there is even some broad agreement about the need for redistribution to remedy past injustice. However, domestic redistribution raises fears about reducing the opportunities for the formerly privileged groups, especially with regard to future generations. And the strategy of solving distributive problems through growth, rather successfully employed by North European social democracies during the 1950s and 1960s, today faces a less favourable international environment for variations on economic policy.

Current European modernity from a South African point of view

The preceding remarks are aimed at opening a reflection – certainly only a beginning – on South African democracy as a new *mise en forme* of society in post-apartheid South Africa (broadly following Claude Lefort). They focused on three socio-political questions that have in general accompanied the history of modernity but for which South Africa shows a strong particularity. First, the idea of collective autonomy requires a collectivity capable of deliberating about its own rules and laws, and this is particularly difficult when such a collectivity emerges from a former situation in which a minority oppressed and excluded the majority of the same collectivity. Second, any modern polity needs to determine the relation between individual autonomy and collective autonomy, between the freedom to self-determine one's own life and the freedom to collectively shape the conditions in which good lives – in variety – can be lived. Debates during past decades have led to an emphasis of the former over the latter in the West. This turn may be problematic in its own way in western societies, as this author would hold. For South Africa, it is highly plausible to maintain that the creation of the conditions for living good lives needs so considerable a collective effort that any easy acceptance of the 'western turn' to prioritize individual self-realization seems precluded. This applies in particular, thirdly, to the conditions of poverty that prevail for almost half of the South African population and to the conditions of highly unequal access to the benefits that a society is basically capable of providing, such as health care and basic and higher education, as they suggest that this society does not exist as a collectivity of responsibility.

If our reflections were to end on this note, we would risk after all giving the impression that South African modernity is similar to western, apparently universal, modernity, but imperfectly or less developed. To avoid this misunderstanding – which should have been precluded by the terminology adopted, but can all too easily arise – an addition is required. West European modernity – to limit ourselves to this part of the West – is assumed not only to have solved all the above issues but to have institutionalized the solutions so that they will be forever safely available. The solutions are, first, the democratic nation-state, in which the homogeneity of the nation paves the way for the emergence of a general, collective will in popular sovereignty; second, the liberal constitutional state of law, which combines the commitment to individual liberty with constitutional guarantees, thus eternalizing the liberal achievement and limiting the power of potentially tyrannical majorities; and thirdly, the welfare state institutionalizing social solidarity by redistributing the surplus generated by the smoothly managed functioning of a market economy.

The point here is not to suggest that these were not achievements. In some significant sense, they were – despite all possible reconsideration and critique. The point is to see them as historical responses to problems arising in a particular form in European settings, thus neither as general solutions nor as permanent achievements whose superiority resides in their conceptual foundations. The temporary nature of these solutions can be recognized by making two further observations, a historical one and one on the current situation, building further on our preceding analysis of the changing relations between capitalism and democracy in Europe (chapter 5). Historically, the solutions were basically all already at hand when European modernity transformed into the totalitarianisms of the post-First World War period. Some of their elements were even used for this transformation, such as the ideas about the unity of the nation and the historical role of working-class solidarity. Others, such as the ideas of individual rights and constitutional guarantees, were insufficient to defend the achievements of modernity in Europe at that moment in history. Today, again, one cannot be too sure about the permanent nature of the features of European modernity. The reach of the general will in its national expression is questioned, both by infra-nation-state movements and the process of European political integration. The relation between individual and collective autonomy is at stake anew when the position of one's own collectivity in the global context needs to be determined. Furthermore, the emphasis on individual liberty reaches conceptual limits in new debates about cultural rights, ethical issues and the ecological sustainability of a way of living in which consumption is seen as a major expression of individual self-realization. Thirdly, the 'European social model' is under strain, due to heightened global competitiveness that limits the surplus to be distributed.

Conclusion

There have been strong connections – conceptual and historical – between western modernity and South African modernity throughout the past two centuries. Despite the fact that South African modernity differed very strongly from the western version in certain periods – in particular between 1948 and 1990 – there has never been such a divide that would suggest the impossibility of using a common basic socio-political conceptuality. Neither did apartheid South Africa step far outside what western moderns were only too willing to accept shortly before or even during the reign of apartheid, nor did western moderns succeed in arresting all further conceptual change because of their accomplishment in putting modernity on secure conceptual and institutional foundations.

Following such reflections, furthermore, the relation between violence and justice will need to be cast in different terms. Defenders of western modernity – like Rorty – often seem to assume that modernity is the regime in which every claim to power and authority is institutionalized in such a way that it acquires justification through its institutional setting. Violence, in turn, while not absent, is being exercised only against those inside or outside who do not accept justified institutional practices. Historically, however, as briefly discussed, European world domination was achieved thanks to a combination of violence, in the form of which Europeans had gained superiority, and new normative claims that indeed were compelling, even though not spelt out in generally applicable terms. This combination transformed South Africa from the eighteenth century onwards into the particular colonial setting in which apartheid grew: a regime of violent domination.

The end of apartheid meant an end to this form of violence. Institutional practices now have to abide by the Constitution that is based on the principles of equal liberty, as in many other polities of the world. Rorty may have thought of this phenomenon: that the range of what can be said and done about politics is very limited once self-government is in place because self-determined practices escape general conceptualization.[17] The effective commitment to individual and collective autonomy, therefore, can be seen as exposing socio-political life in an unprecedented way to needs for justification, to demands for justice in one way or another. In turn, the resort to violence is in principle unjustified. Thus, one may want to consider that the move from a situation of partial heteronomy, as under apartheid, towards autonomy as 'modernization' may be the only defensible use of this term after the critique of sociological modernization theory from the 1960s onwards.

Even if one accepts such terminology, though, there is neither an end to conceptual change (not even 'conceptual

---

[17] As Gordon Wood (1969) noted about the beginnings of the American Republic. This phenomenon may be mirrored in the disappearance of critical debate, of critical sociology in particular, in South Africa after the end of apartheid. Critique mobilizes sophisticated conceptual apparatuses to explain and overcome persistent violent situations, but this repertoire is of little use once self-government is the logic that determines institutional practice (see Gumede and Dikeni 2009 and Katito 2010 for analyses of contemporary South Africa in this light; and Vale 2010 for a brief reconstruction of the role of the humanities in shaping South African self-understanding).

revolutions' are excluded in the future) nor an end to the need for social analysis.[18] The modern commitment to individual and collective autonomy, as I think I have demonstrated elsewhere (most recently, Wagner 2008), is widely open to a diversity of interpretations. My comparative reflections on post-apartheid South Africa and Europe gave an indication of currently different situations and different conceptual stands on how to best interpret them with a view to solving urgent problems. In conclusion, it shall just be suggested, first, that differences of interpretation are not normally due to 'backwardness', not even in the sense of lack in one setting of an experience already had in another setting, but may reflect a genuine difference in situation; and second, that there is no reason to suggest that future interpretations of modernity may not bring forth new conceptual approaches in an attempt to solve new kinds of problem. Rather, the

[18] The generalized need for justification under conditions of modernity does not mean the end of violence; rather, it means that violence is itself in need of justification and can be denounced as unjustified. Political struggle under modern conditions is often in the first place a struggle over the most suitable interpretation of a situation (see Karagiannis and Wagner forthcoming a). When such struggle, though, is inconclusive and cannot be ended by procedural means (such as a vote or a verdict) either, defenders of an interpretation resort to other means – means that are often violent in a broader or stricter sense of the term, including market power, media power, or illicit use of police power. This holds for domestic situations; in inter-state and inter-society relations, which are not ordered by any generally accepted law, resort to violence in the narrow sense of the term is common. When, to take a recent and well-known example, former US President George W. Bush could not win the struggle over an adequate interpretation of the situation in Iraq, he resorted to military means without justification. More generally, the current post-colonial situation, where formal equality exists between states in the international order, is frequently marked by the violent imposition of terms of trade and 'terms of communication' that persist over extended periods.

current global condition of modernity seems to require such unprecedented interpretations.

There is, furthermore, at least one topical reason why South Africa is a place of particular interest when looking at novel interpretations of modernity. When the European powers first occupied Africa, they imposed their administration while at the same time allowing only very limited access to the 'metropolitan' institutions – we may describe as 'global apartheid' the situation that prevailed from the late nineteenth century until decolonization and the formalization of specifically South African apartheid after the Second World War. Subsequently, in response to calls for independence, or what I call here collective self-determination, Europeans allowed 'separate development' in the African form of the nation-state, while maintaining economically highly unequal relations, not determined by market position but by legal and political measures, selectively creating or barring access to political and individual opportunities, including market access. South Africa's combination of a recent move towards inclusive egalitarian democracy while maintaining structures of social inequality makes it a mirror image of a world situation in which independent states, on a formally equal basis, negotiate policy measures for a sustainable future but in which at the same time asymmetries of power and wealth are extremely pronounced, due to the legacy of the 'great divergence' that produced a world dominated by the West. South Africa's internal 'great divergence' is historically and conceptually linked to the still persistent, even though attenuated, great divergence in the world. South Africa may even be seen today as more 'advanced' than much of the world because there is no legal or political barrier any longer between its citizens – as there is, in contrast, between citizens of Senegal and France, or Nigeria and the United Kingdom, or Tanzania and Germany. The problematic attempts at self-determined collective action to overcome the inequality in South Africa are therefore of particular interest elsewhere where belief in collective action and planned change has subsided to a great extent.

8

Towards a World Sociology of Modernity

The preceding suggestions for a social and political theory and a comparative sociology of modernities have come a long way which it will be useful to retrace before adding one final element to my reasoning, a sketch of the requirements for, and basic assumptions of, a future world sociology of modernity.

In an opening step, I have underlined the fact that modernity has always been conceived of as containing universal commitments, the validity of which was claimed for the whole world (chapter 1). Even though these commitments have discernible local origins in the form in which we have come to know them, it was assumed that they would diffuse across the world by virtue of their superiority to other claims and commitments. Such an assumption has faced increasing criticism over the past half-century, upon which we have touched at various points. In a second step, however, I have chosen to focus on a recent transformation in the self-understanding of modernity that is at the core of all prior debate: rather than being a stable accomplishment, modern forms of socio-political organization have started to undergo major changes over the past few decades; and one of the consequences of these changes is that it has become obvious over the past two centuries that there may be a plurality of such modern forms of which one cannot easily say that any one embodies the commitments of modernity better than the others (chapter 2).

These insights have engendered new questions: if modernity can continue changing radically and exist in a variety of forms, what does that mean for our idea of progress? I have tried first to answer this question by reviewing the historical transformations of European modernity in the light of possible criteria of progress, thus staying with a notion of progress as improvement over time and postponing the normative comparison of contemporaneous modernities (chapter 3). I addressed social progress in terms of inclusion and individualization, material progress as better satisfaction of human needs, and political progress as enhancement of the capacity to solve problems through collective action. My conclusion was that progress exists and remains possible, but is by no means certain; rather, it is endangered on all those fronts. Up to this point, I have continued to employ a rather comprehensive concept of modernity, even though the distinction of dimensions of progress was a step towards the disentangling of components of modernity, deemed necessary in order to be able to compare contemporaneous modernities across space rather than time. The final step in re-theorizing modernity consisted in the elaboration of a concept of modernity that does not presuppose large and stable collectivities held together by common meaning and/ or coercive institutions, such as societies or civilizations, but instead focuses on social processes of communication that provide a collective self-understanding (chapter 4).

The second part of these reflections tried to put the insights gained in the first part to work. In a first step, I investigated the historically changing relations between the ways human beings have chosen to address the economic and the political *problématiques* of modernity, increasingly so as forms of capitalism and democracy (chapter 5). The conclusion was that European modernity had recently undergone a democratic crisis of capitalism and that this crisis is at the heart of the recent transformation of modernity. Slightly more speculatively, I explored whether this specific, historical crisis can be seen as an expression of a basic underlying tension between possible solutions to the economic and political *problématiques* under conditions of modernity. To explore this latter question further and to embed the prior insights in a larger picture, I extended this investigation beyond Europe, a step that required a reflection on varieties of colonial situations to extend the overly narrow horizon of the multiple modernities debate. Thus, we have been able to transform the question of modernity into one of a comparative-sociological investigation of the current global constellation. My specific choice of looking in depth at 'new societies' founded in the aftermath of European colonization, such as Brazil and South Africa, allowed us to recognize the state of connectedness within the world at around 1800 as a particularly crucial moment in the formation of varieties within global modernity (chapters 6 and 7).

Sociologically, modernity – and more recently 'globalization' – has often been described in terms of time–space compression (most explicitly, Harvey 1991). Without giving particular theoretical or definitional significance to this term, it is undoubtedly fruitful to connect the experience of modernity to ways of situating human lives in time – in its most basic sense, to be modern means to be in one's own time – and extending relations to others in space.[1] In this sense, recent time–space compression facilitated by information, communication and transport technologies has certainly increased the interconnectedness of social practices across the world, a key theme of recent globalization debate. The current state of the world would be misunderstood, however, if we looked at it from the angle of self-propelled processes of an evermore extensive network of social relations. Rather,

---

[1] Reinhart Koselleck's (1979) felicitous characterization of the change in European political languages between 1770 and 1830 as distancing the horizon of expectations from the space of experience, as mentioned above, expresses a temporal statement in a spatial metaphor.

such analysis should be a preparatory step towards under-standing the worldliness of the world, to paraphrase Hannah Arendt again; that is, to see how far extended social practices are experienced and interpreted by the human beings who enact them in the world that they inhabit together. Thus, our attempt to rethink modernity with a view to understanding the present will conclude with some brief observations on how an investigation of the contemporary condition of modernity would need to situate the modern experience in time and space.

Space (1): multiple modernities and our relation to the axial age

The theorem of multiple modernities addresses the current plurality of modern forms of socio-political organization by resorting to the claim of a long-lasting parallel unfolding of different cultural programmes (see chapters 2 and 4 above for some discussion). This is an understandable move, trying to escape the impact of technological or, more generally, functional determinism, which has shaped much sociological debate about modern societies from the early nineteenth century onwards. It is unfortunate, nevertheless. The objec-tive of arguing for persistent plurality is thus achieved, but the historical origins of the claim tend to fall into oblivion, and this may be the moment to recall them.

With all their topicality, Shmuel Eisenstadt's analyses are grounded on a reconsideration of the so-called axial age, the period between roughly 700 and 400 BCE, around which, according to the original philosophical version, world history turns, separating pre-history from history. Most basically, the axial age hypothesis today suggests that parallel and somewhat similar major socio-cultural transformations occurred in several regions of Eurasia during that period (see Arnason, Eisenstadt and Wittrock 2005 for a comprehensive reassessment). In the view of current interpreters, these trans-formations significantly inaugurated a distinction between a mundane sphere of human action and a transcendental sphere; furthermore, they may also have been the origins of the classic world civilizations whose 'cultural programmes' crystallized in the aftermath of the axial age, namely the Chinese, Japanese and Hindu ones, with developments in the Eastern Mediterranean region being complicated by the fact that Judaism and Greek philosophy contributed to the axial age, but Christianity and Islam occurred later in, as some authors term it, 'secondary breakthroughs'. There is ongoing debate about the nature and meaning of the axial age (see Wagner 2005 for my view). For current purposes, only one aspect needs to be singled out: the axial age hypothesis needs to affirm some, even though thin, interconnectedness between the regions in question, as otherwise the co-occurrence of rather similar social transformations would be a highly unlikely coincidence. Thus, a more adequate version of the multiple modernity theorem would place less emphasis on the separate and different origins of various cultural pro-grammes, and consequently some fundamental diversity between contemporary modernities, and would focus instead on the long-term interconnections in world history that not only permit historico-sociological comparison but also suggest that there may be some proximity, or family resem-blance, between the basic *problématiques* that human beings have tried to address collectively at various places and points in time.[2]

Let us illustrate the matter with one example that is of concern both to social theory and to current global debate: the question of the individual and his or her rights. In topical debate, we see here the confrontation between a concept of human rights that is considered to have western origins and at the same time universal significance, the latter being evidenced, for instance, by the existence of a Universal

---

[2] Bearing in mind that such proximity of *problématiques* does not warrant a return to the idea of universal perennial problems for which straightforward conceptual solutions are to be sought, rightly criticized by Quentin Skinner (1988 [1969]).

Declaration of Human Rights adopted by the United Nations. At the same time, there is an ongoing debate in which some authors regard non-western self-understanding as lacking a concept of the individual and/or as embedding individuals too strongly in the collectivities of which they are members, whereas others maintain that the concept of human rights is open to a variety of interpretations and the western one is only one of those, which furthermore is not necessarily superior to others.

One way of opening up this debate is to recognize that the concept of the individual as the basic unit of social ontology has never been unanimously accepted in western debates. Trying to summarize the conceptual debate, the agreement resides rather in the recognition that there are physical human beings who necessarily entertain social relations with others, and the controversy is about the degree to which these physical human beings should be conceptually separated, as knowing and acting subjects, from their environment, including other human beings, or, in turn, the degree to which their connectedness with others defines their way of being 'individuals'. Put like this, the difference between western and non-western conceptions shrinks; at the very least, there is no longer an unbridgeable divide. Following debates within Hindu and Islamic cultures about the key concepts of *dharma* and *umma*, one recognizes a similar *problématique* that is addressed in different terms. Most importantly, as Santos (2007: 16–21; see above, chapter 3) underlines, one will recognize the incompleteness and the weaknesses of 'one's own' conception when trying to understand those that have emerged in different historical and cultural backgrounds. Thus, the recourse to the axial age may indeed help to explain current cultural difference, in the profound sense of different ways of being-in-the-world, and its persistence. However, its assertion of broadly similar historical occurrences also serves to underline 'translocal intelligibility' and the possible 'recognition of reciprocal incompletenesses' (Santos 2007: 17–18) due to the long-term connectedness of human history.

Time (1): from the ancients to the moderns

In a very general sense, and keeping the limits of our knowledge in mind, the axial-age transformations can be seen as a period of profound self-questioning and as the conscious introduction of new ways of interpreting the world at a moment of crisis. It is not common parlance to refer to the social configurations that emerged from these transformations as modern, with the partial exception of Athenian democracy (see Arnason, Raaflaub and Wagner forthcoming), but it is worthwhile reflecting further on their modernity, with all its limits, and in particular on the modernity of the transformations themselves (Wagner 2005).

The idea of any strong and direct connection between the axial-age social configurations and those of our present era cannot be sustained. No such relation is assumed between Greek democracy or the Roman Republic and present-day Europe (for recent discussions, see Meier 2009; Wagner 2010), and thus western thinkers should be cautious in suggesting any such continuity for other 'civilizations', such as the Chinese one, which may emerge only because of ignorance of the finer details of Chinese history. On the other hand, the alternative assumption of radical discontinuity, as promoted for instance by Aldo Schiavone (1996), only begs further questions. Even if we allow for radical reinterpretations, we need to account for the facts that western socio-political language derives many of its key concepts from ancient Greek and that Continental European juridical institutions operate on the basis of canonized rules that are known as Roman law. In other words, a long historical perspective on the history of modernity should focus on the central question of the relation between 'the ancients and the moderns' as one neither of straight continuity nor of radical discontinuity. Those authors who contributed to formulating that distinction, such as Benjamin Constant in 1819, were after all not drawing a sharp line of separation but were investigating degrees of difference and similarity.

In other words, we may say that the ancients addressed *problématiques* that stay with us. We will no longer want to address them in the same way as the ancients did, but we will need to address them in some way, and a return to the ancients may provide us with interpretative resources to find solutions adequate to the way the *problématiques* present themselves under current circumstances. I will try to briefly illustrate the issue by pointing to the three key *problématiques* of modernity that were defined earlier (chapter 4).

The distinction between a mundane and a transcendental sphere that, according to Eisenstadt, the axial-age transformations inaugurated has tended to be interpreted along the lines that the monotheistic religions suggested. In their view, we live in this world but have knowledge gained through revelation of another world, and this knowledge of another world can guide our actions in the present, in this world. This interpretation is useful for a comparative history of religion and to some extent for a sociology of religion today. However, it does not exhaust the meaning of the axial-age innovation, and another interpretation may be more suitable for understanding our modernity and its epistemic *problématique*. Namely, the distinction between such two spheres more generally creates a difference between 'reality' as we experience it and another possible world – or worlds – that we can imagine. The imagined existence of those other worlds then provides us with the means to criticize 'reality'. In this way, the axial-age distinction inaugurates the possibility of critique and its use as a tool for change (see chapter 3 above for this terminology, derived from Luc Boltanski's discussion of critique).

Secondly, the conception of freedom that emerged during the democratic era of ancient Greece has a highly ambivalent status in our time. It is referred to as the source of our understanding of personal freedom, and thus our autonomy and our modernity. But it is also critically discussed and ultimately rejected because the personal freedom of male citizens of Athens was connected to their high commitment to the political order, such that their duties in the service of collective autonomy outweighed personal liberties in a way that is deemed unacceptable in our time. While this may even be true, our hermeneutic distance from the ancient *polis*, combined with a scarcity of information, will not allow us to adjudicate the matter in a definitive way. It is much more important to recognize that the *polis* citizens were committed to both personal freedom and collective self-determination and that they had a sense of the necessary – and fragile – connection between the two that often gets lost in current debates (see Karagiannis and Wagner forthcoming b). One of the key concerns of the political *problématique* of modernity remains the balance between individual and collective autonomy. And as earlier discussions suggested (see in particular chapters 6 and 7), there is no reason to assume that the correct such balance could be found once and for all. Rather, modernities may differ in this regard, and their situations may change over time so that they may want to alter this balance (as discussed in chapter 3).

Thirdly, the socio-political fact that most separates us from the ancients is slavery and the denial of citizenship to women and slaves (though we still deny citizenship to resident aliens). This difference, though, should be considered as a challenge to make comparison possible across the divide. In the terms developed above, the ancient Greeks pursued a highly modern approach to the political *problématique*, but they excluded categories of persons from this commitment to autonomy. This exclusion was justified by a conceptual distinction between political matters, which were amenable to freedom of speech and action, and economic matters, which were governed and determined by the necessities of life. As women and slaves were dealing with those necessities, they provided the conditions for autonomy in political matters, but were at the same time deprived of exercising this autonomy (Wagner 2008, ch. 5; Arendt 1958 developed a similar interpretation).

In this light, new interpretations of our modernity emerge, along with new questions. The idea of a self-regulated market economy can be seen as enlarging the concept of autonomy to also cover economic matters. However, as we have seen (chapter 5), the viability of such an idea was soon in question, and the relation between political self-determination and economic self-determination has remained in debate. Furthermore, the emergence of political economy and subsequently of the economic sciences undermines the interpretation of market self-regulation as autonomy. It implies, namely, that market interactions and their outcomes are governed by laws, and are thus determined and not free. Finally (a question we alluded to at the end of chapter 5), the distinction between people who are free and others who deal with necessities may not have disappeared at all. In the current world, millions of people take care of the necessities of others but are deprived of participating in determining the rules for the life in common. The distance between the ancients and our contemporary selves remains an urgent topic of investigation.

Space (2): 1800 – European modernity or modern world-making?

The years around 1800 are often considered to be the period of the origins of European modernity. There is no need to deny or downplay the major transformation that European societies started to undergo in the mid- to late eighteenth century nor the crucial impact that European developments would have on socio-cultural transformations worldwide. For some time, historians of Europe have concentrated on more subtle analyses of the period between 1770 and 1830, dispelling the notion of 'great transformations'; and postcolonial scholars have questioned the normative and functional significance of the difference between Europe and other regions of the world. While there is no doubt that many such works have contributed significantly to our understanding of history, the question of the specificity of Europe does not therefore go away. And now, as the result of cumulative research over the past three decades, we may be able to address it in different terms.

We can identify two main flaws in prior reasoning. First, the underlying assumption was that change happened endogenously in Europe and then diffused across the world. Second, the specificity of Europe was seen in cumulative events during the so-called early modern period, from 1500 to 1800, leading to the breakthrough of modernity around 1800. Now we can say with good reason that the change that occurred in Europe was dependent on Europe's relations with other parts of the world; and that the great divide occurred in the nineteenth century, not earlier. These insights emerge from recent works in 'world history', and we have discussed earlier the seminal work by Kenneth Pomeranz (2000), which underlines the similarities across several regions of the world before 1800 and explains the later economic change in Europe as overcoming a restraint resulting from global trade, and the synthesis by C. A. Baily (2004), who, building on Pomeranz, discards the view that earlier European innovations in science and philosophy, political, legal or economic institutions were decisive for the divergence in development during the nineteenth century. These findings support the notion that European powers started to dominate the world in the nineteenth century, but they allow and require us to rephrase some of the issues that this entails.

First, the diffusion of modernity has been explained by theorists of modernization and development as being triggered by the performative superiority of a functionally differentiated society. This is a view that we can now discard. In Talcott Parsons's own writings (see, e.g., Parsons 1964), however, the argument is presented in a less forceful way than his followers often assumed. Drawing on the analogy with natural selection, Parsons leaves considerable space for 'survival' of a variety of 'species' due to insulation or identification of 'niches'. Introducing more recent ecological concerns, one can go further and suggest that diversity is an asset in its own right, given the greater probability of adaptation to changed circumstances. But we should not carry the analogy too far, as social change in human societies is reasonably seen as quite distinct from natural selection. Staying closer to historical evidence, we recognize that elites in some societies perceived European developments as a challenge to which they needed to respond (see Kaya 2004), and the analysis of such attitudes allows us to speak about 'advance' in different ways than conceptually determined functional or normative superiority.

Such debates about the need for 'westernization', for instance, emerged in the Russian and the Ottoman Empires, both bordering on Europe. In the early eighteenth century, though, the Russian view focused on military and administrative technology, state centralization in particular, that is, the technologies of power and not the benign innovations that Europeans used to give central place to in the account of their own progress. Towards the end of the nineteenth century, related debates emerged in China and Japan, though the degree of confidence in one's 'own' institutions and culture was higher than in the aforementioned cases. The outcome of these 'encounters' (to use again Talal Asad's term) arguably altered the trajectory of the non-European societies, but it is not fruitfully to be seen as either westernization or the assertion of a long-standing cultural programme but rather as a selective perception, active interpretation and modified introduction of certain features of 'European modernity' in the given context.

Second, the need for adaptation because of European military superiority might be seen as a special case of the perceived higher performance of the West. It is a very special case, however, because the encounter is here determined by the risk of military defeat and possibly extinction, not by any feature of the West that is regarded as worthy of emulation in its own right. The European colonizers had without doubt the higher 'firing power' and many colonial encounters were determined by this difference. The history of South Africa provides a good illustration as neither the Dutch nor the British settlers were initially aiming for colonization in the narrower sense of the term, that is, the occupation of the territory and domination over the local population. The Dutch settlers invaded the territory further only when exposed to stronger British settlement and domination in the coastal trading posts, and even then their encounters with the native African population were limited to those parts of the territory that they occupied for agricultural purposes. The African societies resisted successfully for a considerable time, and historians do not detect any economic superiority of the colonizers that determined the outcome of the encounters. Rather, the viability of African polities and their trade and agriculture was purposefully undermined and destroyed when they entered into competition with the settlers, and this destruction was powered by military might (Thompson 2006).

Finally, the diffusion of European modernity can also be seen as due to the normative attractiveness of the principles of individual and collective self-determination. Under the long reign of more materialist explanations of history, including modernization theory, during the latter half of the twentieth century, such views were rarely heard, but they are coming more strongly to the fore nowadays since the language of 'human rights and democracy' returned to the core of contemporary self-understanding. Indeed, many occurrences in the late eighteenth and nineteenth centuries can be interpreted in this light as assertions of the principle of collective self-determination, most significantly in the Americas with first the (North) American and Haitian declarations of independence and subsequently the creation of independent states in South America. Such 'founding of new societies' (Hartz 1964) against the background of earlier colonization was clearly inspired by the modern imaginary as it had been developed in Europe, but again we cannot speak of a case of simple diffusion. The newly founded societies displayed a breadth of interpretations of modernity that again needs to be understood by the encounter of already different European 'fragments', to use Hartz's term, with different native populations. Current studies of varieties of such non-European modernities can build on the presence of the modern imaginary from those founding moments onwards and will then need to reconstruct the subsequent historical trajectories as reinterpretations of the form of that imaginary adopted at the outset (see, e.g., Chakrabarty 2000; Larrain 2007; Santos 2007).

In sum, the moment of 1800 is, in global perspective, not the beginning of the diffusion of European modernity but rather the onset of parallel processes of world-making, inspired by the modern imaginary but pursued under conditions of considerable power differentials.

Time (2): 1880s–1960s – a global organized modernity

In this context, the particularity of the United States of America resides in the fact that its foundations, at the origins, were rather symmetrically erected on both individual and collective autonomy, indeed giving preference to the former over the latter. The principle of collective self-determination strongly informed all founding of new societies as a move towards independence from the colonial powers, but the commitment to, and interpretation of, the principle of individual autonomy varied highly, both in terms of its inclusiveness and the distinction between economic and political liberties. Since oppression on grounds of religion was a major reason for the early North American settlers to leave Britain, the commitment to religious freedom became a cornerstone of the self-understanding of the United States as a society committed to the freedom of individual expression, as lastingly confirmed in the Bill of Rights added to the US Constitution. Elsewhere, in Europe and in many new societies, the liberal modern imaginary informed political debates in a pivotal manner but hardly ever reigned supreme for extended periods before the 1970s.

In Europe, as described in more detail elsewhere (Wagner 1994; see also chapters 5 and 7 above), the liberal imaginary was first restricted by means of the exclusion of large strata of the population, in a formal way by limiting civic rights and political participation, in more informal ways through restricted access to 'modern' economic and cultural practices. As the imaginary provided the resources for the transcendence of those 'original' limitations, a major line of internal critique of modernity demanded full inclusion (see chapter 3 above). Such inclusion had been by and large accomplished by the first inter-war period through organizing modernity around collective concepts such as, most importantly, nation and class, at the expense, however, of channelling the expressions of individual liberty into large-scale organizations, as a 'secondary' means of containing the reach of the modern imaginary.

Looking beyond Europe, we can recognize how colonial domination became the global concomitant to the 'original' restrictions of liberal modernity. In analogy to eighteenth- and nineteenth-century views of women and workers, European property-owning male thinkers clearly recognized that special justifications were required to exclude groups of human beings from modernity once the latter's imaginary was accepted, and a variable mix of biological, socio-structural and historical reasons were invoked to explain why Africans, in particular, were not able to shoulder the responsibility that goes along with the recognition of their full autonomy. An educational view of the relation between the Europeans and the colonized was created, employing parental, domestic concepts of responsibility for beings that, though human, were still in a state of minority. In parallel, European action towards the colonized was seen in terms of efficient intervention to enable 'development' following an industrial model of mastery and control. Such discourse prevailed until the 1970s in European development policy documents, that is, far into the era of decolonization, in the name of collective self-determination (Karagiannis 2004).

Time (3): 1970s–the present – globalization as the destructuring of organized modernity

Contemporary South African society struggles to overcome its apartheid heritage, its very particular interpretation of organized modernity. Social inequality and residential segregation are not easily removed, even by a majority party that is firmly in power and has an efficient state apparatus at its disposal for policies of transformation. Furthermore, apartheid is part of the lived experience of the 'coloured' and 'black' population of South Africa that cannot be negated or denied without the risk of depriving experiences and the memory of them of any reasonable significance. Jacob Dlamini's *Native Nostalgia* (2009) analyses life in a township under apartheid by calling it to memory, including his own. Such memory is not without fondness, and the – liberal–democratic – present by no means always compares favourably with a past marked by oppression and exclusion. In this respect, it resonates with European or North American nostalgic longings for the orderly world of the 1950s and 1960s that withered away in the face of individualization and globalization, as current sociological and journalistic jargon has it.[3]

European organized modernity faced gradual de-conventionalization from the late 1960s onwards. This process accelerated at the end of the 1970s when a sense of more profound crisis had built up, and further de-conventionalization became the policy agenda of governments rather than merely the unintended outcome of numerous uncoordinated actions and processes (see chapter 5 above). The more or less negotiated collapse of a partial world order between 1989 and 1992, namely the fall of Soviet socialism, required a response in terms of institutional rebuilding, and the temporary intensification of European integration can be seen as part of this response. At the time of writing, however, it has become clear that this response was both half-hearted and insufficient, not least because it took global developments too little into account. Described in this way (see chapter 7

---

[3] In some respects, the book may be compared with Edgar Reitz's monumental film *Heimat*, evoking German everyday life under Nazism and during the 'restorative' early post-Second World War period.

above), European history during the past half-century looks less dissimilar to the South African one than we are used to believing. Significantly, it also suddenly looks much less successful. It rather seems as if South Africans, like many global Southerners today, who start out from much more problematic social, economic and sometimes political conditions than Europeans and other Northerners, have a better grasp of the dimensions of current global change and its impact on their societies and are collectively more determined to address them.

This remains to be seen. Behind this observation, though, lurks a question that needs to be raised. Throughout this book, I have employed – more or less explicitly at different moments – a comparison between the 1960s and the present with a view to better understanding our present. It is clear that the sociological ways of understanding the present of the 1960s exuded a much greater confidence of grasping reality than our current ways. Sociologists then thought that they had the means to explain 'modern society', and that this society was indeed basically stable and predictable, Today, 'modernity' seems in constant flux, one crisis following another, and the events that trigger them have not been predicted and have even sometimes been ruled out, and in evermore cases crises do not get resolved but remain as a burden on collective action capacity when yet new problems arise.

This is the context in which the term 'progress' gets redefined as regress, as Claus Offe proposed, and in which one fears losing grip on changing reality that would permit its critique and the imagination of another world, as Luc Boltanski surmised (chapter 3 above). However, such views, which have emerged strongly in what we may call the metropolitan, Northern left, or a certain generation of it, are profoundly problematic. Ultimately, they rest on the intuition that the organized modernity of the second half of the twentieth century so much embodied our ways of living and thinking that its dismantling requires a retreat from earlier convictions and the – nostalgic, to be sure – abandonment of the normative and conceptual principles that had marked progressive, critical thinking for two centuries or more.

Was, however, the defence of the organized modernity of the 1960s ever an option? Is its demise mainly due to the disassociation of capitalist practices from nation-state democracies, as diagnosed above (chapter 5)? European organized modernity demonstrated considerable accomplishments by, say, 1970 – it is not difficult to agree with Offe on this issue. However, the seeds of its demise came from two sources besides capital. The conventions of organized modernity were challenged from inside by calls for greater freedom of self-expression on the one hand. And, on the other hand, European-organized modernity by 1970 was possibly the last institutionalization of European (better, western) global domination. Its accomplishments were based on selectively closing the doors to the South and thus continue to benefit from the sedimented results of colonialism at the moment of the latter's formal end. If we add these insights to the picture, we will understand the greater determination of the South to address the *problématiques* of modernity in their current guise. And we will also recognize that our inherited categories have not been superseded; they are in need of reinterpretation.

Space (3): the global present – rethinking freedom, equality and solidarity

The preceding observations should have suggested that, 'globalization' being far from an entirely novel phenomenon, we have lived in a highly common world for two and a half centuries, if not millennia, even though we have interpreted it in a wide variety of ways at different times and in different places. Sociologically, the transformations of this world should be analysed in terms of changing structures and extensions of social relations – authoritative, allocative and ideational ones – and the preceding analysis should have given some ideas and concepts as to how this – enormously difficult – task can be addressed and possibly accomplished.

Such analysis, even if pursued in a flawless way, will gain its full significance only, however, if it is set in the context of the modes of normative philosophy that have accompanied modernity with great explicitness over the past two and a half centuries and in a more implicit or indirect way over much longer periods. To conclude, three brief remarks in terms of a reappraisal of the normative commitments of the French Revolution shall suffice.

It may be true, first, that individual liberty has never had such a prominent place in world history as it has now. Major theoretical efforts have been made to separate – liberate, some may want to say – the idea of individual freedom from conceptual contexts that were seen as endangering its full meaning. Time and again, however, it has also been observed that such attempts have had the opposite effect: by abstracting freedom, to paraphrase Hegel's terminology, from the practical contexts in which free action can only be meaningful, some conceptual purification was possibly achieved but at the price of losing all significance and relevance (Wagner 2008: chs 2 and 11). 'Globalization' spells the weakening of meaning-providing contexts, and as such it may create new spaces for 'individualization'. But such apparent normative gain, to return to Honneth's criteria of progress (above, chapter 3), may occur against the background of the weakening of inclusion-providing institutions and their accompanying modes of recognition.

That is to say, the inclusion-providing institutions of organized modernity operated – and arguably needed to operate – with clear and strong boundaries of eligibility or membership. Organized modernity showed some achievements in terms of domestic justice and equality, but it had no means of addressing the global situation beyond the boundaries of a given state. Second, to phrase the issue of equality and justice in a slightly provocative way, we may ask under what conditions a theory of 'separate development', the justificatory pillar of the apartheid regime, is justifiable. The separate organization of modern nations in the name of self-determination is not as far away from 'separate development' as defenders of modernity are inclined to think. The nation-state model was built on the implicit assumption that those states were equal and were also equal providers of justice to their members. In practice, though, this was clearly often not the case. Inside nation-states, the relations between the English and the Scottish, or between North and South Italians, were relations of inequality and domination. Among nation-states, this was similarly the case between, for instance, Sweden and Finland, or Great Britain and Portugal or Argentina.

We have to recognize that normative 'separation' is justifiable at best in the pronounced absence – or thinness, to use a common metaphor – of economic, political and cultural ties between the members of the respective entities. Whenever there are significant such ties, considerations of justice need to cross the boundaries of these entities. Coming back to the example, the apartheid notion of 'separate development' was at best somewhat defensible before gold and diamond mining, and the oppressive laws accompanying it, forced large numbers of black Africans into the economy and society of the dominant white groups – and this means before any such ideas were even formulated. Once such hierarchical division of labour on highly unequal terms had emerged and consolidated, no justification of separateness was defensible any longer. In turn, we have to ask whether the current global division of labour has not created a density of economic ties across the world that requires the urgent development of concepts and practices of global justice (see Ypi 2008 for a constructive proposal).

Such latter development will need to be underpinned by a novel understanding of the ties that make human beings commit themselves to considering the fate and destiny of other human beings. Reinterpreting older understandings that referred to such ties as friendship, pity or brotherhood, the early nineteenth-century socio-cultural transformations in Europe witnessed the emergence of the novel term 'solidarity', for which claims of superiority over the older terms soon emerged. Solidarity was supposedly built on equality, not paternalistic hierarchy; on abstraction, not proximity; and on reason, not passion. Despite those claims, though, the term found its transposition into concrete historical forms in versions of national solidarity and class solidarity, as well as its institutional translation into the welfare state. Thus, it came to refer too closely to the social configuration of organized modernity to be of unmodified use in the global present. The current destructuring of organized modernity requires anew a 're-specification of the social bond with a political view' (Karagiannis 2007, on which the above draws) of the kind that was achieved during the nineteenth century but capable of creating and maintaining the world in the face of the current risk of worldlessness.

References

Adorno, Theodor W. (1986 [1937]) 'Neue wertfreie Soziologie? Aus Anlass von Karl Mannheims "Mensch und Gesellschaft im Zeitalter des Umbaus"', *Gesammelte Schriften 20(1), Vermischte Schriften I*, Frankfurt/M: Suhrkamp, pp. 13–45.

Adorno, Theodor W. and Horkheimer, Max (1997 [1944]) *Dialectic of Enlightenment*, London: Verso.

Agamben, Giorgio (1995) *Homo sacer: Il potere sovrano e la nuda vita*, Turin: Einaudi.

Aglietta, Michel (1979 [1976]) *A Theory of Capitalist Regulation: The US Experience*, London: New Left Books.

Alexander, Jeffrey C. (1978) 'Formal and substantive voluntarism in the work of Talcott Parsons: A theoretical and ideological reinterpretation', *American Sociological Review* 43, 177–98.

Almond, Gabriel A. and Verba, Sidney (1963) *The Civic Culture: Political Attitudes and Democracy in Five Nations*, Princeton: Princeton University Press.

Arendt, Hannah (1958) *The Human Condition*, Chicago: University of Chicago Press.

Arnason, Johann P. (1989) 'The imaginary constitution of modernity', in Giovanni Busino et al. (eds), *Autonomie et autotransformation de la société: La philosophie militante de Cornelius Castoriadis*, Geneva: Droz, pp. 323–37.

Arnason, Johann P. (2003) *Civilizations in Dispute*, Leiden: Brill.

Arnason, Johann P. (2010) 'Interpreting Europe from East of centre', in Johann P. Arnason and Natalie Doyle (eds), *Domains and Divisions in European History*, Liverpool: Liverpool University Press.

Arnason, Johann P., Eisenstadt, Shmuel and Wittrock, Björn (eds) (2005) *Axial Civilizations and World History*, Leiden: Brill.

Arnason, Johann P., Raaflaub, Kurt and Wagner, Peter (eds) (forthcoming) *The Greek Polis and the Invention of Democracy: a Politico-cultural Transformation and its Interpretations*, Oxford: Blackwell.

Asad, Talal (1995) *Anthropology and the Colonial Encounter*, New York: Prometheus,

Avritzer, Leonardo (2007) 'Modes of democratic deliberation: participatory budgeting in Brazil', in Boaventura de Sousa Santos (ed.), *Democratizing Democracy*, London: Verso, pp. 377–404.

Baily, C. A. (2004) *The Birth of the Modern World, 1780–1914*, Oxford: Blackwell.

Bauman, Zygmunt (1987) *Legislators and Interpreters*, Cambridge: Polity.

Bauman, Zygmunt (1989) *Modernity and the Holocaust*, Cambridge: Polity.

Bauman, Zygmunt (1991) *Modernity and Ambivalence*, Cambridge: Polity.

Bauman, Zygmunt (2000) *Liquid Modernity*, Cambridge: Polity.

Beck, Ulrich (1986) *Risikogesellschaft*, Frankfurt/M: Suhrkamp.

Beilharz, Peter (2008) 'Australian settlements', *Thesis Eleven* 95: 58–67.

Berman, Marshall (1982) *All That is Solid Melts into Air: The Experience of Modernity*, New York: Simon and Schuster.

Boltanski, Luc (1990) *L'amour et la justice comme compétences*, Paris: Métailié.

Boltanski, Luc (1993) *La souffrance à distance*, Paris: Métailié.

Boltanski, Luc (2009) *De la critique*, Paris: Gallimard.

Boltanski, Luc and Chiapello, Eve (1999) *Le nouvel esprit du capitalisme*, Paris: Gallimard.

Boltanski, Luc and Thévenot, Laurent (1991) *De la justification*, Paris: Gallimard.

Boltanski, Luc and Thévenot, Laurent (1999) 'A sociology of critical capacity', *European Journal of Social Theory* 2(3) (August): 359–77.

Boudon, Raymond (1984) *La place du désordre: Critique des théories du changement social*, Paris: Presses universitaires de France.

Buchmann, Marlis (1989) *The Script of Life in Modern Society: Entry into Adulthood in a Changing World*, Chicago: University of Chicago Press.

Burke, Edmund (1993 [1790]) *Reflections on the Revolution in France*, Oxford: Oxford University Press.

Butler, Anthony (2010) 'The African National Congress under Jacob Zuma', in John Daniel et al. (eds), *2010: Development or Decline? New South African Review* 1, Johannesburg: Wits University Press, pp. 164–83.

Castells, Manuel (1996) *The Rise of the Network Society*, Oxford: Blackwell.

Castoriadis, Cornelius (1975) *The Imaginary Institution of Society*, Cambridge, MA: MIT Press.

Castoriadis, Cornelius (1990) *Le monde morcelé: Les carrefours du labyrinthe III*. Paris: Seuil.

Chabal, Patrick (2009) *Africa: The Politics of Suffering and Smiling*, Scottsville: University of KwaZulu-Natal Press.

Chakrabarty, Dipesh (2000) *Provincializing Europe: Postcolonial Thought and Historical Difference*, Princeton: Princeton University Press.

Chakrabarty, Dipesh (2009) 'The climate of history: four theses', *Critical Inquiry* 35 (Winter): 197–222.

Coetzee, J.M. (1991) 'The mind of apartheid: Geoffrey Cronjé (1907–)', *Social Dynamics* 17(1): 1–35.

Coetzee, J.M. (1996) 'Apartheid thinking', ch. 9 in Coetzee, *Giving Offense: Essays on Censorship*, Chicago: University of Chicago Press.

Connell, Raewyn (2007) *Southern Theory: The Global Dynamics of Knowledge in Social Science*, Cambridge: Polity.

Crozier, Michel, Huntington, Samuel and Watanuki, Joji (1975) *The Crisis of Democracy: Report on the Governability of Democracies to the Trilateral Commission*, New York: New York University Press.

Daedalus (1998) 'Early modernities', 127(3) (summer).

Daedalus (2000) 'Multiple modernities', 129(1) (winter).

Didry, Claude and Wagner, Peter (1999) 'La nation comme cadre de l'action économique. La Première Guerre mondiale et

174 *References*

l'émergence d'une économie nationale en France et en Allemagne',
in Bénédicte Zimmermann, Claude Didry and Peter Wagner
(eds), *Le Travail et la nation: Histoire croisée de la France et de
l'Allemagne*, Paris: Editions de la Maison des Sciences de
l'Homme, pp. 29–54.

Dlamini, Jacob (2009) *Native Nostalgia*, Johannesburg: Jacana.

Domingues, José Mauricio (2006) *Modernity Reconstructed*,
Cardiff: University of Wales Press.

Domingues, José Mauricio (2008) *Latin America and Contemporary
Modernity: A Sociological Interpretation*, London: Routledge.

Domingues, José Mauricio (2012) *Global Modernity Development
and Contemporary Civilization: Towards a Renewal of Critical
Theory*, London: Routledge.

Eisenstadt, Shmuel Noah (2002) *Multiple Modernities*, Piscataway,
NJ: Transaction.

Eisenstadt, Shmuel Noah (2003) *Comparative Civilizations and
Multiple Modernities*, Leiden: Brill.

Ewers, Adalbert and Nowotny, Helga (1986) *Über den Umgang
mit Unsicherheit*, Frankfurt/M: Suhrkamp.

Ferry, Luc and Renaut, Alain (1988) *La pensée 68*, Paris: Seuil.

Foucault, Michel (1984), 'What is enlightenment?', in Paul Rabinow
(ed.), *The Foucault Reader*, London: Penguin, pp. 32–50.

Fourie, Elsje (forthcoming) 'Does modernity still matter? Evaluating
the theory of multiple modernities and its alternatives',
*Social Science Information/Information sur les sciences
sociales*.

Fraser, Nancy and Honneth, Axel (2003) *Redistribution or
Recognition? A Political-Philosophical Exchange*, London:
Verso.

Galtung, Johan (1975) *Strukturelle Gewalt: Beiträge zur Friedens-
und Konfliktforschung*, Reinbek bei Hamburg: Rowohlt.

Gerschenkron, Alexander (1962) *Economic Backwardness in
Historical Perspective*, Cambridge, MA: Harvard University
Press.

Gevisser, Mark (2009) *A Legacy of Liberation: Thabo Mbeki and
the Future of the South African Dream*, New York: Palgrave
Macmillan.

Giddens, Anthony (1984) *The Constitution of Society*, Cambridge:
Polity.

Giddens, Anthony (1990) *The Consequences of Modernity*,
Cambridge: Polity.

Giddens, Anthony (1994) 'Living in a post-traditional society', in Ulrich Beck, Scott Lash and Anthony Giddens (eds), *Reflexive Modernization*, London: Sage.

Glyn, Andrew and Sutcliffe, Bob (1972) *British Capitalism, Workers and the Profit Squeeze*, Harmondsworth: Penguin.

Gramsci, Antonio (2011) *Prison Notebooks*, New York: Columbia University Press.

Gumede, William and Dikeni, Leslie (eds) (2009) *The Poverty of Ideas: South African Democracy and the Retreat of Intellectuals*, Auckland Park: Jacana.

Habermas, Jürgen (1968) *Technik und Wissenschaft als Ideologie*, Frankfurt/M: Suhrkamp.

Habermas, Jürgen (1973) *Legitimationsprobleme im Spätkapitalismus*, Frankfurt/M: Suhrkamp.

Habermas, Jürgen (1981) *Theorie des kommunikativen Handelns*, Frankfurt/M: Suhrkamp.

Habermas, Jürgen (1985) *Der philosophische Diskurs der Moderne*, Frankfurt/M: Suhrkamp.

Habermas, Jürgen (1990) *Die nachholende Revolution: Kleine politische Schriften, vol. VII*, Frankfurt/M: Suhrkamp.

Habermas, Jürgen (1998) *Die postnationale Konstellation*, Frankfurt/M: Suhrkamp.

Hall, Peter A. and Soskice, David (2000) (eds), *Varieties of Capitalism*, Oxford: Oxford University Press.

Hartz, Louis (1955) *The Liberal Tradition in America: An Interpretation of American Political Thought*, New York: Harcourt, Brace, Jovanovich.

Hartz, Louis (1964) *The Founding of New Societies: Studies in the History of the United States, Latin America, South Africa, Canada, and Australia*, San Diego: Harcourt, Brace, Jovanovich.

Harvey, David (1991) *The Condition of Postmodernity: An Enquiry into the Conditions of Cultural Change*, Oxford: Blackwell.

Hedström, Peter and Wittrock, Björn (eds) (2009) *Frontiers of Sociology*, Leiden: Brill.

Henningsen, Manfred (2009) *Der Mythos Amerika*, Frankfurt/M: Eichborn.

Hirschman, Albert (1977) *The Passions and the Interests*, Princeton: Princeton University Press.

Hirschman, Albert (1991) *The Rhetoric of Reaction: Perversity, Futility, Jeopardy*, Cambridge, MA: Belknap Press of Harvard University Press.

Hirschman, Albert O. (1993) 'Exit, voice and the fate of the German Democratic Republic: An essay in conceptual history', *World Politics* 45(2): 173–202.

Holston, James (2008) *Insurgent Citizenship: Disjunctions of Democracy and Modernity in Brazil*, Princeton: Princeton University Press.

Honneth, Axel (1992) *Kampf um Anerkennung*, Frankfurt/M: Suhrkamp.

Honneth, Axel (2004a) 'Gerechtigkeit und kommunikative Freiheit. Überlegungen im Anschluß an Hegel', in Barbara Merker, Georg Mohr and Michael Quante (eds), *Subjektivität und Anerkennung: Festschrift für Ludwig Siep*, Paderborn: Mentis, pp. 213–27.

Honneth, Axel (2004b) 'Organized self-realization: some paradoxes of individualization', *European Journal of Social Theory* 7(4): 463–78.

Honneth, Axel (2005) *Verdinglichung: Eine anerkennungstheor-etische Studie*, Frankfurt/M: Suhrkamp.

Honneth, Axel (2009) 'Das Gewebe der Gerechtigkeit. Über die Grenzen des zeitgenössischen Prozeduralismus', *Westend: Neue Zeitschrift für Sozialforschung* 6(2): 3–22.

Joerges, Christian, Stråth, Bo and Wagner, Peter (eds) (2005) *The Economy as a Polity: The Political Constitution of Contemporary Capitalism*, London: UCL Press.

Jubber, Ken (2007) 'Sociology in South Africa: A brief historical review of research and publishing', *Sociology* 22(5): 527–46.

Kalyvas, Andreas (2005) 'Popular sovereignty, democracy, and the constituent power', *Constellations* 12(2): 223–44.

Karagiannis, Nathalie (2004) *Avoiding Responsibility: The Politics and Discourse of EU Development Policy*, London: Pluto.

Karagiannis, Nathalie (2007) 'Multiple solidarities', in Nathalie Karagiannis and Peter Wagner (eds), *Varieties of World-making: Beyond Globalization*, Liverpool: Liverpool University Press.

Karagiannis, Nathalie (2010) 'Democracy as a tragic regime', *Critical Horizons* 11(1): 35–49.

Karagiannis, Nathalie and Wagner, Peter (eds) (2007) *Varieties of World-making: Beyond Globalization*, Liverpool: Liverpool University Press.

Karagiannis, Nathalie and Wagner, Peter (2008) 'Varieties of agonism: conflict, the common good and the need for synagonism', *Journal of Social Philosophy* 39(3) (Fall): 323–39.

Karagiannis, Nathalie and Peter Wagner (forthcoming a) 'Political imagination and tragic democracy', to be published in a special issue of *Critical Horizons*, titled 'Political Imaginaries' and edited by Suzi Adams, Jeremy Smith and Ingerid Straume.

Karagiannis, Nathalie and Wagner, Peter (forthcoming b) 'The liberty of the moderns compared to the liberty of the ancients', in Johann P. Arnason, Kurt Raaflaub and Peter Wagner (eds), *The Greek Polis and the Invention of Democracy: A Politico-cultural Transformation and its Interpretations*, Oxford: Wiley-Blackwell.

Katito, José (2010) *Sociology in South Africa*, MA thesis, University of Trento, Faculty of Sociology.

Kaya, Ibrahim (2004) *Social Theory and Later Modernities: The Turkish Experience*, Liverpool: Liverpool University Press.

Koselleck, Reinhart (1959) *Kritik und Krise*, Freiburg: Alber.

Koselleck, Reinhart (1979) *Vergangene Zukunft*, Frankfurt/M: Suhrkamp.

Krog, Antjie (1998) *Country of My Skull: Guilt, Sorrow, and the Limits of Forgiveness in the New South Africa*, New York: Random House Broadway.

Krog, Antjie (2009) *Begging to be Black*, Cape Town: Random House Struik.

Lake, Marilyn (2008) 'Equality and exclusion: the racial constitution of colonial liberalism', *Thesis Eleven* 95: 20–32.

Larrain, Jorge (2000) *Identity and Modernity in Latin America*, Cambridge: Polity.

Larrain, Jorge (2007) 'Latin American varieties of modernity', in Nathalie Karagiannis and Peter Wagner (eds), *Varieties of World-making: Beyond Globalization*, Liverpool: Liverpool University Press, pp. 41–58.

Lefort, Claude (1986) 'La question de la démocratie', in *Essais sur le politique: XIXe–XXe siècles*, Paris. Seuil, pp. 17–30.

Lefort, Claude (1999) *La complication*, Paris: Fayard.

Lijphart, Arend (1975) *The Politics of Accommodation: Pluralism and Democracy in the Netherlands*, Berkeley: University of California Press.

Lipton, Merle (2007) *Liberals, Marxists and Nationalists: Competing Interpretations of South African History*, New York: Palgrave Macmillan.

Lyotard, Jean-François (1979) *La Condition postmoderne*. Paris: Minuit (trans. G Bennington and B. Massumi (1994) *The*

Postmodern Condition, Manchester: Manchester University Press).

Majone, Giandomenico (1996) *Regulating Europe*, London: Routledge.

Mann, Michael (1993 [1986]) *The Sources of Social Power*, 2 vols, Cambridge: Cambridge University Press.

Mbembe, Achille (2001) *On the Postcolony*, Berkeley: University of California Press.

Meier, Christian (2009) *Kultur, um der Freiheit willen. Griechische Anfänge – Anfang Europas?* Munich: Siedler.

Meiksins Wood, Ellen (1996) 'Modernity, postmodernity or capitalism?', *Monthly Review* 48(3) (July/August): 21–39.

Meiksins Wood, Ellen (1999) *The Origin of Capitalism*, New York: Monthly Review Press.

Morse, Richard M. (1964) 'The heritage of Latin America', in Louis Hartz (ed.), *The Founding of New Societies*, San Diego: Harcourt, Brace, Jovanovich, pp. 123–77.

Mota, Aurea (2010) 'The attenuated liberal constitutional proposal in Latin America'. Paper presented at the International Social Theory Consortium Conference, University of Sussex, June.

Myrdal, Gunnar (1944) *An American Dilemma: The Negro Problem and Modern Democracy*, New York: Harper.

Narr, Wolfdieter and Offe, Claus (eds) (1975) *Wohlfahrtsstaat und Massenloyalität*, Cologne: Kiepenheuer und Witsch.

Noiriel, Gérard (1991) *La tyrannie du national*, Paris: Calmann-Lévy.

Offe, Claus (1998) 'Demokratie und Wohlfahrtsstaat: eine europäische Regimeform unter dem Streβ der europäischen Integration', in Wolfgang Streeck (ed.), *Internationale Wirtschaft, nationale Demokratie*, Frankfurt/M: Campus, pp. 99–136.

Offe, Claus (2009) 'Political disaffection as an outcome of institutional practices? Some post-Tocquevillean speculations', in André Brodocz et al. (eds), *Bedrohungen der Demokratie*, Wiesbaden: VS, pp. 42–60.

Offe, Claus (2010) 'Was (falls überhaupt etwas) können wir uns heute unter politischem "Fortschritt" vorstellen?', *Westend: Neue Zeitschrift für Sozialforschung* 7(2): 3–14.

Outhwaite, William (2005) *The Future of Society*, Oxford: Blackwell.

Parsons, Talcott (1964) 'Evolutionary universals in society', *American Sociological Review* 29(3) (June): 358–74.

Pocock, J.G.A. (1975) *The Machiavellian Moment*, Princeton: Princeton University Press.

Polanyi, Karl (1985 [1944]) *The Great Transformation*, Boston: Beacon.

Pomeranz, Kenneth (2000) *The Great Divergence: China, Europe, and the Making of the Modern World Economy*, Princeton: Princeton University Press.

Raaflaub, Kurt A. (forthcoming) 'Perfecting the "political creature" (*zōion politikon*): equality and "the political" in the evolution of Greek democracy', in Johann P. Arnason, Kurt Raaflaub and Peter Wagner (eds), *The Greek Polis and the Invention of Democracy: A Politico-cultural Transformation and its Interpretations*, Oxford: Blackwell.

Rawls, John (1971) *A Theory of Justice*, Cambridge, MA: Belknap Press of Harvard University Press.

Ribeiro, Darcy (1971 [1969]) *The Americas and Civilization*, New York: Dutton.

Rorty, Richard (1989) *Contingency, Irony, Solidarity*, Cambridge: Cambridge University Press.

Rueschemeyer, Dietrich, Stephens, Evelyne Huber and Stephens, John D. (1992) *Capitalist Development and Democracy*, Chicago: University of Chicago Press.

Salais, Robert and Storper, Michael (1993) *Les Mondes de production*, Paris: Editions de l'EHESS.

Santos, Boaventura de Sousa (ed.) (2006/7) *Reinventing Social Emancipation*, 3 vols, London: Verso.

Santos, Boaventura de Sousa (2007) 'Human rights as an emancipatory script? Cultural and political conditions', in Santos (ed.), *Another Knowledge is Possible: Beyond Northern Epistemologies*, London: Verso, pp. 3–40.

Scharpf, Fritz (1999) *Governing in Europe: Effective and Democratic?* Oxford: Oxford University Press.

Schiavone, Aldo (1996) *La storia spezzata*, Rome/Bari: Laterza.

Schmidt, Volker H. (2010) 'Modernity and diversity', *Social Science Information* 49(4): 511–38.

Schwartzman, Simon (1991) 'Changing roles of new knowledge: research institutions and societal transformations in Brazil', in Peter Wagner et al. (eds), *Social Sciences and Modern States*, Cambridge: Cambridge University Press, pp. 230–60.

Seekings, Jeremy and Nattrass, Nicoli (2006) *Class, Race, and Inequality in South Africa*, Durban: University of KwaZulu-Natal Press.

Sewell, William H., Jr (1980) *Work and Revolution in France*, Cambridge: Cambridge University Press.

Sewell, William H., Jr (1994) 'Ideologies and social revolutions: reflections on the French case', in Theda Skocpol (ed.), *Social Revolutions in the Modern World*, Cambridge: Cambridge University Press, pp. 169–98.

Sewell, William H., Jr (1999) 'Three temporalities: towards an eventful sociology', in Terrence J. McDonald (ed.), *The Historic Turn in the Human Sciences*, Ann Arbor: University of Michigan Press, pp. 245–80.

Sewell, William H., Jr (2005) *Logics of History: Social Theory and Social Transformations*, Chicago: University of Chicago Press.

Skinner, Quentin (1988 [1969]) 'Meaning and understanding in the history of ideas', in James Tully (ed.), *Meaning and Context: Quentin Skinner and His Critics*, Cambridge: Cambridge University Press, pp. 29–67.

Skocpol, Theda (1979) *States and Social Revolutions*, Cambridge: Cambridge University Press.

Skocpol, Theda (1994) 'Cultural idioms and political ideologies in the revolutionary reconstruction of state power: a rejoinder to Sewell', in Skocpol (ed.), *Social Revolutions in the Modern World*, Cambridge: Cambridge University Press, pp. 199–209.

Smelser, Neil (1997) *Problematics of Sociology*. Berkeley: University of California Press.

Sombart, Werner (1920) *Der Bourgeois: Zur Geistesgeschichte des modernen Wirtschaftsmenschen*, Berlin: Duncker and Humblot.

Stoeckl, Kristina (2011) 'European integration and Russian Orthodoxy: Two multiple modernities perspectives', *European Journal of Social Theory* (May) 14: 217–33.

Taylor, Charles (1989) *Sources of the Self*, Cambridge, MA: Belknap Press of Harvard University Press.

Taylor, Charles (2005) *Modern Social Imaginaries*, Durham, NC: Duke University Press.

Thomas, Lynn M. (2011) 'Modernity's failing, political claims, and intermediate concepts', *American Historical Review* (June): 1–14.

Thompson, Leonard M. (1964) 'The South African dilemma', in Louis Hartz (ed.), *The Founding of New Societies*, San Diego: Harcourt, Brace, Jovanovich, pp. 178–218.

Thompson, Leonard (2006) *A History of South Africa*, Johannesburg and Cape Town: Ball.

Touraine, Alain (1992) *Critique de la modernité*. Paris: Fayard.

Vale, Peter (2010) ' "Silencing and worse ...": the humanities and social sciences in South Africa', in John Daniel et al. (eds), *2010: Development or Decline? New South African Review* 1, Johannesburg: Wits University Press, pp. 261–80.

Wagner, Peter (1994) *A Sociology of Modernity: Liberty and Discipline*, London: Routledge.

Wagner, Peter (1999) 'After *Justification*: Repertoires of evaluation and the sociology of modernity', *European Journal of Social Theory* 2(3) (August): 341–57.

Wagner, Peter (2001) *Theorizing Modernity*, London: Sage.

Wagner, Peter (2005) 'Palomar's questions: the axial age hypothesis, European modernity and historical contingency', in Johann Arnason, Shmuel Eisenstadt and Björn Wittrock (eds), *Axial Civilizations and World History*, Leiden: Brill, pp. 87–106.

Wagner, Peter (2008) *Modernity as Experience and Interpretation: A New Sociology of Modernity*, Cambridge: Polity.

Wagner, Peter (2010) 'Europe – what unity? Between political philosophy and historical sociology', in Johann P. Arnason and Natalie Doyle (eds), *The Unity and Diversity of Europe,* Liverpool: Liverpool University Press.

Wagner, Peter (2011) 'The future of sociology: understanding the transformations of the social', in Charles Crothers (ed.), *The History and Development of Sociology*, Paris: UNESCO and EOLSS.

Wagner, Peter (forthcoming) 'World-sociology beyond the fragments', in Saïd Amir Arjomand (ed.), *Social Theory and Regional Studies in the Global Age*, Albany, NY: SUNY Press.

Wagner, Peter, Hirschon Weiss, Carol, Wittrock, Björn and Wollmann, Hellmut (eds) (1991) *Social Sciences and Modern States: National Experiences and Theoretical Crossroads*, Cambridge: Cambridge University Press.

Walzer, Michael (1983) *Spheres of Justice*, New York: Basic Books.

Walzer, Michael (1988) *The Company of Critics, Social Criticism and Political Commitment in the Twentieth Century*, New York: Basic Books.

Walzer, Michael (2001) *Che cosa significa essere americani*, 2nd edn, Padua: Marsilio.

Weber, Max (1949 [1904]) ' "Objectivity" in social science and social policy', in Edward E. Shils and Henry A. Finch (eds), *The Methodology of the Social Sciences*, New York: Free Press, pp. 50–112.

Wittrock, Björn (1983) 'Governance in crisis and the withering of the welfare state: the legacy of the policy sciences', *Policy Sciences* 15(3): 195–203.

Wood, Gordon (1969) *The Creation of the American Republic, 1776–1787*, Chapel Hill, NC: University of North Carolina Press.

Yack, Bernard (1997) *The Fetishism of Modernities*, Notre Dame, IN: University of Notre Dame Press.

Ypi, Lea L. (2008) 'Statist cosmopolitanism', *Journal of Political Philosophy* 16(1): 48–71.

Index

abortion 46, 100, 135
Adorno, Theodor W. 6–7,
    18, 57, 62, 86
African-Americans 110
African National Congress
    (ANC) 131–2, 136–7,
    138, 140–2
Afrikaner 112, 114, 127
Agamben, Giorgio 66
agriculture 104, 127, 162
alienation 7, 17–18, 20, 46,
    48, 51, 87, 98
apartheid ix, 10, 34, 105,
    114–15, 120–4, 128,
    130–49, 164–5, 168–9
Arab societies viii, 108
Arendt, Hannah 62, 66,
    129–30, 153
Argentina 169
Aristotle 93
Arnason, Johann P. xiv,
    32, 67–8
Aron, Raymond 8
Asad, Talal 161
'Asian values' 33

atomism 66
atomization 20
Australia 25, 126
Austria 89
autonomy 43, 61, 158–9, 164
    collective 99, 138
    individual 7, 17–18, 33, 42,
        44, 47, 62, 82–3, 142,
        157, 163
    and mastery 18, 20, 22, 128
    relation between individual
        and collective 30, 41–2,
        77, 101, 144, 147–8, 158
    undermining of 23
axial age 61, 153–7

Baily, C. A. 109, 125, 160
barbarism 54–5
bare life 66
Bauman, Zygmunt 8, 13, 35
Beck, Ulrich 13, 20, 35–6
Bell, Daniel 8
Boltanski, Luc 38, 43, 51,
    57–62, 83, 157, 166
Boudon, Raymond 56

Bourdieu, Pierre 57, 65, 135
Brazil ix, xiii, 25, 78, 100,
    103, 105–6, 108, 111–15,
    118, 137, 152
Bretton Woods agreement
    97
Burawoy, Michael 56
Burke, Edmund 54
Bush, George W. 148

Cape Town 133, 139,
    142
  District Six 133
capitalism
  in Brazil 114
  capitalist modernization,
    paradoxes of 58
  capitalist society, as concept
    13, 15, 57
  and critique 19, 38, 51,
    60, 63
  and democracy x–xii,
    81–106, 151–2
  as economic modernity 9,
    82–3
  global viii
  and mastery 61
  network 47
  and organized modernity
    167
  in South Africa 130, 134,
    138
  spirit of 7, 91, 99
Castoriadis, Cornelius 22,
    61, 73
Chandler, Alfred 91
Chiapello, Eve 38, 51, 60
China viii–ix, 14, 94, 103,
    108, 161
  Chinese civilization 24,
    154, 156

Christianity 113, 154
  Calvinism 113,
  Protestantism viii, 7, 14,
    108
  Thomism 113
citizen
  demands of 86
  disaffection 82, 96, 98,
    100–1, 103, 137
  freedom of 10
  and non-citizens 105
  rights-holding 135
citizenship 76, 105, 115–16
  Athenian 157
  European 104
  exclusion/inclusion 46, 114,
    149
civilization(s)
  analysis of 24–5, 32, 64–8,
    71, 73, 77, 108, 116, 151
  classic 126, 154, 156
  and modernity 6, 33
Cold War 122, 132
commerce, freedom of 41–2
commodification 7, 20, 44
communitarianism 110
conformism 46–7
Constant, Benjamin 156
consumer society 49
convergence theorem 11, 24,
    26, 81
cosmopolitanism 102
creativity 7, 99
  and agency 21, 24, 118
  collective 69–70, 77
crisis
  of capitalism viii, 49, 82,
    85, 92, 97, 99, 102, 106,
    133, 139, 151–2
  and critique 25, 32, 35–8,
    48, 55, 60–1

of the European sciences 129
financial 101, 103
of governability 87, 91, 98, 132, 134
of modernity 37, 118, 156, 165–6
of South African state 137
'world-crisis' (1780–1820) 109
Critical Theory (Frankfurt School) 18, 56–7, 59, 62, 86
critique/criticism
of capitalism 38, 51, 93, 99
of 'collective concepts' 66, 69, 135–6
and crisis 32, 35–8, 48, 157, 166
of modernity 6–7, 10, 13, 17–20, 23, 40, 58, 65–6, 131, 164
of modernization theory 64, 69, 111, 119, 147

decolonization viii, 130, 149, 164
Declaration of the Rights of Man and of the Citizen 4, 47
democracy ix, 115, 135
ancient 73, 156
in Brazil 106, 111–12, 137
and capitalism x–xiii, 8, 81–106, 147
as collective autonomy 75–6
and critique 63
and human rights 120, 162
as political modernity 9, 30, 114–15
in South Africa 106, 111–12, 138–44, 149

Democratic Alliance 142
democratization ix, xiii, 9, 62, 81–5, 89–91, 99, 103, 114, 137
dependency theory 115, 126
Derrida, Jacques 12
Descartes, René 3
Dewey, John 93
dharma 34, 155
divorce 46, 100, 135
Dlamini, Jacob 122, 131, 165
Durkheim, Emile 19, 72, 117
Dutch settlers 112, 127, 161

East Asia 26, 50, 97, 126,
East Asian model 108
ecological debate 51, 101, 146, 160
Eisenstadt, Shmuel N. 6, 15, 24, 31, 61, 153, 157
electrical and chemical engineering viii, 49, 91
enclosures 88
Engels, Friedrich 4, 82
England 84
Enlightenment 3, 7, 17, 21, 40, 56, 61, 84, 109
equality 5, 30, 34, 43, 54
gender 103
international 148
legal 135
justice and 168
political 123, 142, 159
ethnic relations 115–16, 133
Eurasia 61, 153
Eurocentrism 11, 33, 75, 109
European integration 103, 118, 135, 165
Evolutionism 30, 69, 119

exception
  moral 45, 48
  of apartheid South Africa
    121–2, 124, 129
exclusion 122
  apartheid 105, 124, 128,
    131, 140, 142–3, 158,
    165
  cultural 41
  external 47
  political 94, 115, 163
  social 37, 47–8, 115

finance capital 91
financial crisis 99, 101, 103
Finland 169
Ford, Henry 91
Fordism 91, 92, 95
Foucault, Michel 12, 21
France 14, 57, 59, 84, 89, 149
freedom vii, x, 4, 6–8, 16–17,
  21, 23, 37, 40, 43, 56, 86,
  123, 128, 131, 147
  of commerce 5–6, 41–2,
    47, 53, 76, 83, 88, 128,
    163
  of expression 100, 163,
    167
  individual/personal 76,
    145–6, 157, 163–4, 168
  individual and collective 30,
    75, 120, 144, 158
French Revolution 4, 11, 28,
  38, 40, 54, 70–1, 84, 90,
  105, 109, 168
friendship 47, 169
Fukushima 51
functionalism 35, 65, 69, 119

Gagarin, Juri 122
Galtung, Johan 50

Germany 17, 48, 149
  East (GDR) 132
  everyday life 165
  Imperial 91, 139
  language 41, 56
  Weimar 140
  West (FRG) 96
  Nazi 7, 89
Giddens, Anthony 20, 35–6,
  65–6
Gini coefficient 50
globalization 3–5, 9–11, 53–4,
  66, 98–9, 118–19, 152,
  164–5, 168
Goethe, Johann Wolfgang 42
Goldthorpe, John 56
governability 86, 91, 98–9,
  132, 134, 136
Gramsci, Antonio 87, 93
Great Depression 8, 82
Greece 90, 101, 103
  ancient 73, 103, 154,
    156–8

Habermas, Jürgen 12, 31,
  43–4, 53, 65, 76, 84
Haiti 162
Hall, Peter 83
Hartz, Louis 109–10, 127,
  162
Hegel, G. W. F. 15, 45, 48,
  168
Heidegger, Martin 129
Heller, Agnes 117
Hilferding, Rudolf 91
Hirschman, Albert 41, 53, 88,
  132, 135
Honneth, Axel 32, 43–5, 48,
  58, 60, 168
Horkheimer, Max 7, 18, 57,
  86

Human Development Index
122
human rights 4, 31, 33–4, 43,
47, 84, 117, 120, 154–5,
162
Huntington, Samuel 121
Husserl, Edmund 129

imaginary signification 22–4,
73
inclusion 37, 45–7, 52, 106,
114, 117–18, 131, 134,
143, 151, 164, 168
individualization 10, 20, 45,
47–8, 52, 118
Industrial Revolution 3, 11,
17, 49, 84, 86, 88
Second viii, 91
Third viii, 92
industrial society viii, 8, 13,
92
post-industrial society
8, 12
inequality 113,
social ix, 37, 50, 66, 106,
112–13, 136, 140, 149,
159, 164, 168
information and
communication
technology viii, 12, 49,
92, 152
instituting moment 61
Iran viii–ix, 14, 28, 97
Iraq 148
Islam viii, 33–4, 108, 154–5
Israel ix

Japan viii, 14, 24, 51, 97,
107–8, 154, 161
Judaism 154
juridification 44

justice 32, 43–5, 120–1, 125,
146–7, 168–9
global 47, 99, 169
injustice 60, 93, 141
justification 62, 94, 99, 105,
113, 120–1, 125, 131,
133, 146–8, 164, 169

Kant, Immanuel 5
Kaya, Ibrahim 25
Kennedy, John F. 122
Keynesianism viii, 14, 38, 97,
136
Koselleck, Reinhart 28, 61, 152

Latin America ix, 33, 50, 88,
100, 102, 111, 137
Latour, Bruno 39
Lefort, Claude 144
legitimacy 53, 87, 95, 99,
103, 132, 134, 136, 140
liberalism 87, 137, 142
individualist 110
political and economic 85,
94
see also neo-liberal thought
liberty *see* freedom
Locke, John 3, 74
Luxemburg, Rosa 93
Lyotard, Jean-François 8,
11–12, 21, 30

Machiavelli, Niccolo 93
Malmö 133
Malthusian law 49
Mandela, Nelson 132, 139
Mann, Michael 70–2
Mannheim, Karl 62, 86, 93
Marcuse, Herbert 7, 20
market society 81, 85, 128
see also regulation

Marx, Karl 4–6, 9, 17–18, 56, 82–3, 86, 93, 95, 111, 117, 138
mass culture 7
mass production 91, 95, 104
mass society 19, 47, 131
mastery 4, 16–18, 20, 22–3, 27, 61, 128, 164
Mbeki, Thabo 139, 141
Michels, Robert 18
Middle East ix, 82, 98, 127
migration 115
  immigration 46, 104–5
mining 113, 127, 130, 169

nation-state ix, 23, 41, 49, 53, 82, 100, 102, 137, 145–6, 149, 167, 169
national question 128–30
nationalism 41, 129
neo-liberal thought 9, 14, 84, 91, 97–8, 114, 119, 137
neo-modernization 24, 26, 50, 81, 106, 108,
network 47, 70–1, 91, 98, 152
New Zealand 126
Nigeria 149
1968 (student revolt) 7, 97
North America 3, 49, 56, 107, 110, 125, 162–3, 165
Northern Africa 9, 82, 127
Norway 89

Offe, Claus 53–5, 134–5, 166–7
Ottoman Empire 127, 161

Palestine ix
pan-Africanism 126

Parsons, Talcott 6, 12, 21, 24, 70, 76, 86, 161
Patočka, Jan 129
Polanyi, Karl 42, 76, 83, 101
political economy 5, 17, 85, 159
political participation 34, 65, 76, 89, 94, 96, 100, 104–5, 116, 130, 163
political philosophy xi, 8–9, 12–13, 15–16, 21, 31, 38, 42, 61, 85, 113
Pomeranz, Kenneth 160
Portugal 90, 103, 112–13, 169
post-colonial societies 13, 107–9, 111, 126, 146
post-colonial studies 159
poverty 44, 104, 143–4
progress x, xii, 9, 16, 28–57, 64, 123, 125, 161, 166, 168
  social 28–49, 151
  material 49–52, 151
  political 52–5, 135, 151
  and critique 35–8, 55–63

railways 49
rational choice 21, 66
rationalism 5–6, 17, 107
rationality 18, 20–2, 128
rationalization 6, 13, 20, 36
Rawls, John 76, 121
Reagan, Ronald 97
recognition 42–7, 164, 168
regulation
  deregulation 53, 91, 93
  market self-regulation viii, 4, 77, 94, 117, 125, 136, 159
  technocratic re-regulation 102

reification 10, 17, 48, 59
Reitz, Edgar 165
relativism 25, 31–4
religion 33, 108, 113, 133, 164
republicanism 40, 142
revolution 3, 11, 16–17, 30, 40, 84, 86, 140, 148
  American 4
  'catching up' 28
  concept of 28–9
  conceptual 120, 147–8
  cultural (1968) 7
  individualizing 42
  Iranian 14, 113
  Kemalist 25
  market 41, 117
  socialist 95
  see also French Revolution; Industrial Revolution
Rivonia trial 133
Roman Empire and Republic 70, 156
Rorty, Richard 13, 71, 120–1, 146–7
Russia 161,
  Soviet Union 7, 90, 122, 129–30, 132

Santos, Boaventura de Sousa 34, 155
Sartre, Jean-Paul 57
Scandinavia xiv, 97, 105
Schiavone, Aldo 105, 156
Schmitt, Carl 93
Schumpeter, Joseph A. 93
Scotland 84
Senegal 149
serfdom 41–2
Sewell, William H. Jr 70–1, 140

Sharpeville massacre 122–3, 126, 132
Skinner, Quentin 154
slavery 105, 128, 158
Smith, Adam 4
socialism 93, 98, 139
  Soviet vii, ix, 14, 28, 50, 81, 165
society, as a concept 47, 136
solidarity 19, 40, 43, 47, 54, 121, 129, 142–3, 145, 167–70
Soskice, David 83
South Africa ix, xiii, 10, 25, 33–4, 88, 111–49, 161, 164, 166
South Asia 26, 111, 127
South-East Asia 126
South Korea viii–ix, 14, 108
sovereignty 4, 18, 38, 40, 89–90, 99, 116, 125, 141, 145
Soweto uprising 133
Spain 89–90, 101
spirit of capitalism 7, 91, 99
steam engine 49, 88
structural adjustment 98–9
sub-Saharan Africa 108
subjectivity 16, 36
suffrage 4, 18, 89, 93, 114, 116, 138
Sweden 169

Taiwan viii, 14, 108
Tanzania 149
Taylor, F. W. 91, 95
technocracy 102, 118, 133–4
Thatcher, Margaret 97
Thévenot, Laurent 43, 57
Tocqueville, Alexis de 4, 47, 73, 82, 92, 142

totalitarianism 38, 48, 89, 117, 129, 145

Touraine, Alain 13, 20, 35–6, 65, 72

Truth and Reconciliation Commission 112, 141

Turkey 9, 25

umma 34, 155

United Kingdom 84, 97, 149, 169

United States of America ix, 7, 16, 25, 74, 97, 103, 107, 110, 122–3, 130, 134, 136, 163

Universal Declaration of Human Rights 154–5

Bill of Rights (US) 163

universalism 9, 39

urban planning 133

Vietnam War 97

violence 50, 104, 112, 120–5, 131, 139, 141, 146–8

wage labour 5, 17, 41, 83, 88, 95, 99, 105, 130

Weber, Max 5–7, 10, 18, 66, 69, 72, 83, 91, 93, 95, 108

welfare state 18, 38, 87, 101, 106, 130, 136–7, 145, 170

women 46, 123, 131, 135, 158, 164

workers 46, 88, 90–1, 95, 97, 99, 105, 131, 143, 164

World Social Forum 101, 112

world history x, 3, 31, 86, 122, 153–4, 168

as approach in historiography 125, 160

world-systems theory 126

worldlessness 10, 62–3, 170